D0092432

Family-Centered Church

Family-Centered Church

A New Parish Model

Gerald Foley

Sheed & Ward
Kansas City

Copyright© 1995 by Gerald Foley

All rights reserved. No part of this book may be reproduced or transmitted in any form or by any means, electronic or mechanical, including photocopying, recording or by an information storage and retrieval system without permission in writing from the Publisher.

Sheed & Ward™ is a service of The National Catholic Reporter Publishing Company.

———————————————◆———————————————

Library of Congress Cataloguing-in-Publication Data
Foley, Gerald.
    Family-centered church : a new parish model / Gerald Foley.
        p.   cm.
    Includes bibliographical references.
    ISBN: 1-55612-767-7 (pbk. : alk. paper)
    1. Church work with families--Catholic Church. 2. Church work with families--United States. 3. Family--United States. 4. Pastoral theology--Catholic Church. 5. Catholic Church--United States--Membership. I. Title.
    BX2347.8.F3F65 1995
    259'.1--dc20   95-31173
                                                                CIP

———————————————◆———————————————

Published by: Sheed & Ward
                115 E. Armour Blvd.
                P.O. Box 419492
                Kansas City, MO 64141-6492

To order, call: (800) 333-7373

Contents

Introduction

When people talk about life in the family, they speak of love with its abiding presence, its searing pain, its moments of joy and disappointment, its heroic struggle and ordinary routines.[*]

THE UNITED NATIONS DECLARED 1994 THE INTERNATIONAL YEAR of the Family, with the theme, "Family, resources and responsibilities in a changing world." Need to call special attention to the family seems strange when family is always central to who we are. Yet families need to be convinced and supported in their unique role.

Earlier the U.S. Bishops declared 1980-90 as the decade of the family, when all other church ministries were to take a back seat to family ministry, a commitment they renewed for the decade of the 1990s. The response was discouraging.

In 1991, noting that the United States has "the highest divorce rate, the highest teen-age pregnancy rate, the highest child poverty rate and the highest abortion rate in the Western world," the Bishops issued a "call for conversion and action – a spiritual and social reawakening to the moral and human costs of neglecting our children and families."[**] They reaffirmed their call for family ministry in *Follow the Way of Love*, their response to the International Year of the Family.

Michael McManus reflected the failure to know how to achieve effective family ministry and lack of commitment to it in the title of the first chapter of his 1993 book *Marriage Savers*,

---

[*] All chapter epigraphs are taken from the U.S. Bishops' *Follow the Way of Love*.
[**] *Putting Children and Families First: A Challenge for Our Church, Nation and World*.

namely "America's Churches: Part of America's Divorce Problem."*

Noting that "The churches' very access to most American marriages is also a source of great hope," McManus goes on to say that "Churches are ignoring their central pastoral activity: to bond people together in families so that they can withstand the swirling cyclones of a secular world that tear people up and scatter them across the landscape of broken marriages . . . "

Calling for participation in the International Year of the Family, Pope John Paul II urged families to "become what you are." In an environment hostile to family life, who will help them become who they are? The silence in most parishes is astounding. An old axiom reminds us: "If you're not part of the solution, you're part of the problem."

This book suggests some answers, although I do so cautiously, almost reluctantly, because I don't think we need to add more programs so much as to change the mindset of families and pastoral staffs. Programs often pull people away from family life, when families already spend too little time together.

In writing this book, I have often thought of the words of a popular song struggling with love:

> Who can explain it?
> Who can tell you why?
> Fools have all the answers,
> Wise men never try.

My sister once sent me an anniversary card which read: "Thank God for damn fools. Otherwise God's work would never get done!"

My challenge to readers is that, rather than looking for neatly packaged answers here, we dare to be "fools for Christ's sake" (1 Cor. 4:10), believing that with God's help we can still be a source of hope for the families in our parishes. Silence is not an acceptable response. Listening carefully to families seems a wise response before you rush off to start an-

---

* Michael J. McManus, *Marriage Savers* (Grand Rapids, MI: Zondervan Publishing House, 1993).

other program. Those who listen may even rush out to cancel some existing programs.

I hope you will find this book disturbing but helpful.

1

Who Can Explain It?

We know you face obstacles as you try to maintain strong family ties and to follow your calling as a church of the home. The rapid pace of social change, the religious, ethnic and cultural diversity of our society, the revolution of values within our culture, the impact of political and economic conditions: All these place families under considerable stress.

FAMILY LIFE IS MESSY. TO TALK ABOUT FAMILY IS TO TALK ABOUT messy issues like conflict, hurt, mistrust, and the need for reconciliation, as well as busy schedules, diverse interests, and multi-generational worries. Therefore, family ministry is also messy and not neatly packaged. We need to bridge the clutter and chaos of family life with the neat and tidy structure of parish life. Failure to do this makes us try to package family ministry in ways that are not working well, leaving families confused when they find very little in parish family ministry relevant to their needs.

This messiness gets complicated by the uncomfortable issues which reside in family life – subjects like contraception, the changing role of women, sex education, divorce and remarriage, premarital sex and cohabitation. Baffled by these subjects, families get little help from the parish because of the discomfort and possible controversy involved. Family ministers need to listen to and confront uncomfortable and controversial needs as well as comfortable issues.

Families, like parishes, are made up of individuals, but members relate to each other in a complex family system usually overlooked in our ministry. The church orients its spirituality and programs toward the individual. This is consistent with church teaching and the American emphasis on the dig-

nity and rights of the person. It fails to give proper considera-
tion, however, to the interconnectedness of family members
and tends to fragment the life of the family rather than provide support. In contrast, the Charter on the Rights of the
Family clearly states that the rights of the individual have a
social dimension "which finds an innate and vital expression
in the family" (Preamble, A).

We do not need more compartmentalized programs and
ministries today. We need, rather, to rectify this bias by conscious recognition of the family as a system within the larger
systems of the church and society. The church absolutely
needs to address itself to the dimension of relationship, both
in the family and in the parish. If parishes don't care for and
support family relationships, families will look elsewhere for
the support and nourishment they need. Many have already
looked to other groups or denominations.

The family is the church's most basic cell. Parish ministers and volunteer leaders act as if the parish were the primary cell, but that is just not so. Consequently, parish ministers take families for granted. Family ministers frequently
are unmarried and poorly trained for a ministry they barely
glimpse. Yet, single people also participate in messy and
chaotic family life as they relate to their parents and married siblings. Family ministry moves us beyond neat programs to help parents relate to an acting-out teenager or to
help families form support groups for mutual survival.
Healthy relationships are essential to an ecological approach
to society.

Goals of This Book

Why another book on family ministry? I believe parishes
can and must play a major role in supporting family life in the
difficult years ahead. For example, those families involved in
their local church are twice as likely to stay married as those
who are not. Being a family is more a way of thinking about
life than a birth or marriage assignment to a group of people,
more a choice of how life will be than just the place we live.
By family, I include the diversity of family units, all the mir-
acles of "us" that comprise any parish. The changing face of

family life today complicates ministry, often threatening those who would hang onto an unchanging image of what they consider the healthy family.

Most Christians agree on the importance of the family, but we vary on the values we assign to family life. Concern for the family even shapes a major dialogue among politicians. President Reagan contended: "Rebuilding America begins with restoring family strength and preserving family values." Both George Bush and Bill Clinton tried to image themselves as preservers of family life during the 1992 presidential campaign. Mayor Donald Fraser of Minneapolis, a liberal politician for forty years and chairman of our nation's mayors in the early 1990s, admits: "The traditional liberal ideology is out of touch. They have not looked carefully enough at what's been happening to kids and families." Admitting that unmarried pregnancies, family breakdown, and crime continued to multiply while he focused on social programs, Fraser called for a national agenda shaped by a new paradigm which emphasized the "natural systems" of a strong nuclear family and an interdependent community as essential to childrens' development.

I have not attempted a how-to book of programs here. Many good programs are already proposed or active. Rather, I believe current efforts to minister to the family are based on some wrong paradigms or models. The church will achieve its goal of strong family ministry only if some fundamental and difficult changes are made. This, of course, is complicated by rapidly changing times, which demand new and brave approaches.

Some years ago, psychologist Karen Horney warned us that a society which placed almost exclusive value on individual competitiveness and acquisition would de-emphasize and ultimately neglect our needs for love and friendship. In the process of the evolution of "self," we now have an impoverished sense of the "us" and the emotional security that can bring. With our focus on achievement, we consider time even more valuable than money. The average work-week jumped from 41 hours in 1973 to 49 hours in 1987, while companies continued to run on even leaner staffs in the first years of the '90s. In the same years, leisure time declined

32%. VCR's, microwave ovens, fax machines, and fast food drive-throughs remind us that we have little time for each other. Volunteers, who do most of the church's family ministry, now demand tasks they consider important but can do in limited time.

With the advent of what Robert Bellah calls "radical individualism," persons anxious about self-development are less concerned to join a denomination than to find a church that meets their personal needs. A consumer mentality, where people expect multiple options in every area of their lives while demanding quality and service, also means demands on the church. People place minimal trust in large institutions. With the speed of change estimated in the '90s at five times that of the '80s, slow-change institutions will quickly appear obsolete.

Rapid changes will alter the face of the church, testing both its structure and its vision. People value action and results more than credentials or tradition. In a study of what Americans want from their church in the '90s, George Gallup and Jim Castelli found they desire both spiritual and practical services more than doctrine and philosophy in their selection of a church. Admitting to feelings of intense loneliness, people seek community. They expect the church to be a major provider of fellowship and a sense of belonging.

In this need for community, people desire a church life that supports and provides help for families, including single adults and young persons. Americans want churches to help them put their faith into practice, learn how to serve others, and be better parents. They understand their faith will be meaningful only if it has a real impact on their day-to-day lives.

Change is difficult for all of us. We try to shape the future by the past, resisting good ideas that interrupt the status quo, even when these ideas might free us from our limitations and be a source of creative energy. Too often we try to discover and shape the future by looking at it though the old rules and regulations which initially formed our paradigms.

Changing times reflect a change of paradigms from which our actions flow. We can identify some recent paradigm shifts in our culture, such as the change from stress on security to stress on identity, from group goals to individual goals, and from serving the institution to expecting the institution will serve us. We see organizations shifting their paradigms, e.g., from hierarchical and centralized to horizontal and decentralized structures, or from valuing a company person to valuing an entrepreneur. We can even recognize clear paradigm shifts in the church, e.g., from a passive to an active laity and from a maintenance-oriented to a mission-oriented community.

Do I suggest a change of paradigms for family ministry simply as a reaction to changing times? Certainly not. Most persons in previous generations affirmed the family as basic to the well-being of society and church. This consensus, upheld also by church leaders, did not protect the family from today's battering. New insights into human development and family dynamics suggest changes in family ministry. Insights into the need for intimacy and community find better models in the New Testament household churches than in the paternalistic church which shaped our recent ministry. We have John Paul II's warning that the church in the U.S. is too parish-oriented and his challenge to make the family central in all pastoral plans. Our pastoral ministry efforts in recent years have not prevented family breakdown, so perhaps we dare ask, with Mayor Fraser, if "natural systems" hold a better answer.

When we talk about marriage and family in the Catholic Church, we deal with several levels of messages and understanding. On the surface, the church looks like one of the great guardians of marriage and family life. Most would argue that the church ministers from a pro-family paradigm. Yet negative attitudes portraying marriage as a second rate vocation or sexuality as opposed to spirituality, and changing family lifestyles that place many outside the nuclear family and limit the role of laity have led to neglect of marriage and family within the church.

The breakup of the family is the central domestic problem of our time; yet the church's silence on this issue makes it part of the problem. Despite its marriage preparation programs, the church is still more into blessing weddings than creating and sustaining lifelong marriages. The church has stood by silently, watching illegitimacy soar tenfold from 1.7% in 1950 to 17.8% by 1988. Pastors have said little from the pulpit about premarital sex or cohabitation, a cancer eating away at marriage. The number of those living together without marriage increased six-fold between 1970 and 1990, to more than three million couples and over two-thirds of those who marry, even though the *National Survey of Families and Households* reports: "Unions begun by cohabitation are almost twice as likely to dissolve within ten years compared to all first marriages: 57% compared to 30%."* A church that taught about marriage and family life with such certainty finds it difficult to change its pastoral approach. Whenever we change paradigms, past success guarantees nothing. Everyone goes back to zero. Apparent past success now blocks the church's search for new solutions.

A paradigm is a dominant model, our conceptual or experiential explanation of reality. Paradigms exert a powerful influence on the way we see our world, thus they also function as filters to screen information that does not agree with our particular paradigm and exist as a source of prejudice. We select the information that fits our paradigm and then ignore conflicting information. What is obvious to the person with one paradigm is virtually inconceivable to a person with a new or different paradigm. Each of us has many paradigms or maps in our head, both maps of the way things are (realities) and maps of the way things should be (values). We interpret everything we experience through these mental maps, often unaware of having them and seldom questioning their accuracy. These paradigms are the source of our attitudes and behaviors.

We face two obvious effects in changing our paradigms. First, creators of new paradigms are usually found on the margin, outside the institutional framework. Because their vested interest in the old, failed paradigm has diminished, they are motivated to create new paradigms. Secondly, such visionaries show courage because it is not yet certain that the old,

---

* University of Wisconsin, *National Survey of Families and Households,* 1989.

dominant model should be replaced by a new one. They often embrace a new paradigm against all the evidence and in the face of large problems. Such a decision can be made only with faith.

We resist paradigm shifts because they call us to fundamentally reorganize rather than to merely correct the direction we are taking. They challenge us to start with ourselves, taking an inside-out approach, while we tend to favor an outside-in approach focused on how to change others rather than on our ineffectiveness. Then we spend great time and energy establishing rules or programs that force others to shape up so that the problem will be solved.

To emphasize the family rather than the parish as the primary unit of church demands a revolutionary change in the work of parish staffs. To accept the lived experiences of grace in marriage and family life demands that we change from the legal, educational structure of our parishes to a relationship model. As we prepare disciples for their mission, families are no longer objects of the church's ministry and rules, but subjects who find their holiness in living as church in the world rather than in being removed from the world to the protection of Holy Mother Church. They are sacraments whose spirituality builds on living together as lovingly as possible rather than on rules and dogmas.

I suggest family ministry will benefit from the following paradigm shifts, some of which are already underway:

Laity as passive recipients (maintenance)	⟶ Active participants (mission)
Church from parish centered	⟶ Family-centered
Spirituality from	
Individual piety	⟶ Relationships
Disembodied	⟶ Embodied
Otherworldly	⟶ Holiness of ordinary life
Neuter	⟶ Masculine/feminine
Sacramentality from Wedding blessing	⟶ Daily lifestyle
Sexuality from Procreation/mutual love	⟶ Spiritual (Sacramental sign)
Liturgy/Ritual from Institutional	⟶ Home as ordinary place

Fragmenting the Family

The importance of the family to the church is much greater than we realize. The first challenge for family ministers lies in challenging and helping families to discover their own strengths to be healthy domestic units of the church. To be holy means to be healthy and whole in a world where much is unhealthy and fragmented.

Catholics who got excited when Vatican II spoke of the "domestic church" likely had no sense it would be so difficult to change attitudes and practices unsupportive of the family, especially when institutional structures remained unchanged. Even though most Americans view family as one of their highest values, institutions originally created to support families tend to replace them by providing such functions as education, health care, recreation and socialization. These institutions suggest, sometimes not too subtly, that they can perform such functions better than the family can. While giving lip service to the integrity of the family, the church also creates and delivers programs competing with the family.

As parish councils emerged in the post-Vatican II church, advisors suggested standing committees on administration and finance, education, liturgy, social action, and family life. At most diocesan meetings for parish council members, finance, education and liturgy workshops drew crowds, while family ministry was lucky to get a few participants. A bit of hope surfaced when the U.S. bishops approved their Pastoral Plan for Family Ministry in 1978, calling for six categories of ministry to families, namely the engaged, the newly married, parents, marriage enrichment, hurting marriages, and the separated, widowed and divorced. While this plan promised family ministry would dominate the 1980s church, the only major gain helped separated and divorced individuals rather than families.

Most dioceses did set up family life offices, but few parishes, even now, have either family life coordinators or family life committees. What's worse, parish communities unwittingly help pull the family apart. They sponsor men's and women's groups, involve family members in different liturgies, and invite persons to minister as individuals rather than as families. Schools take over the parental task of education. Today's absent generation of baby-boomers reacts indifferently to a church that does not present a compelling theology or stand out from the surrounding culture.

Rearing young adults who will stay in the church and marry other Catholics is no longer the highest priority of Catholic parents. They place a higher value on rearing children who are not addicted, who see a value in marriage over serial relationships, and who emerge with motivation for life. The family finds itself losing out to the peer group and the media in influencing the moral standards of children.

Parish leaders easily try hasty and ill-defined attempts to save the family, which they see in decline. They orient these ministries toward the individualism and fragmentation of family life that permeate our culture, generally failing to address the dimension of relationships or to relate to the family as a system. Much of the attention implies that families are in need of "fixing" by the church or other professionals.

For a long time the church thought it could bypass families. We have little training for marriage and family ministry, yet the task is too important to give to someone without skills. Priests generally acknowledge they have done little to raise their awareness for family ministry since the seminary. Many pastors work as if nothing exists but the church institution. Already overwhelmed by the myriad of parish responsibilities and frustrated by lack of time and energy to accomplish his task, the pastor easily envisions family ministry as an impossible dream. Pastoral staffs often view themselves as the ministers, failing to involve families in like-to-like ministry and unaware that family relationships are central to people's relationship with God.

Listening to families is essential in family ministry. Yet the church generally discounts experience, too often acting as if it has the answers. Families already minister to each other, but require help to see their strengths, to find ways to meet the needs of beleaguered fathers with long commutes to work, mothers feeling a need to apologize for unfinished housework, and children fighting over what to watch on television. Families face many difficult issues, yet they also have the gifts and strengths to develop healthy ministry within and among themselves with the support of the parish church.

Listening will foster innovative rather than static programs. Family ministers have talked a lot lately about a family perspective in the church, i.e., looking at how each of our programs and activities impact the family. Such an awareness is a big step forward, but will not benefit the family significantly until we believe the role of the parish is to strengthen and enhance family life rather than to be an entity to itself. Families are telling us loud and clear that they do not now feel cared for in difficult moments. Friends went to their pastor when their son on drugs was getting into trouble, to be told only "I'm glad I don't have to live with that kid." Other friends, seeking help from their priest for serious marital problems, barely got into the rectory hallway, where the pastor made them kneel and receive his blessing before sending them home to "get along." Many engaged couples have heard their priest comment "I hate weddings" or "I'd rather have ten funerals than one wedding." Such stories abound. We have not taken the family seriously, and both the family and parish suffer for it.

Is There Some Good News?

We all know families feel pressured these days. Prophets of doom continuously predict the end of the family. In *Brave New Families*, Judith Stacey recently concluded: "The 'family' is not here to stay. Nor should we wish it were. On the contrary, I believe that all democratic people, whatever their kinship preferences, should work to hasten its demise." The family, Stacey adds, distorts and devalues "the diverse means by which people organize their intimate relationships."*

As an institution, the family appears in steep decline. In the past 30 years, the divorce rate has tripled. Parents spend increasingly less time with their children and the value placed on children has dropped. By the year 2000, over half of our children are expected to be living in single parent homes. De-

---

* Quoted by David Popenoe, "Don't Believe the Criticism About Two-Parent Families," *Minneapolis Star*, December 31, 1992, p. 19.

linquency, teen-age suicide, child abuse and other problems worsen in families without both parents. We have seen a profound shift in cultural values away from family commitments toward self-fulfillment. Self-gratification has surpassed self-sacrifice. Yet most adults do not seem to be more fulfilled.

As a society, we face many new problems. Not only are we the most marrying and most divorcing country in the world, we are also the most re-marrying. This means many single-parent families face issues of quality child care, balancing work and family and personal time, and struggles with greatly reduced family finances. Blending families also presents unique difficulties.

Women working outside the home reflect one of the most dramatic changes of the twentieth century. Women still remain the primary nurturer in most homes, now balancing household tasks with work while feeling like they carry two full-time jobs. Women who do not work outside the home often feel socially inferior. A longer lifespan now makes the four generation family the norm. These generations frequently do not live anywhere near each other, leaving the elderly feeling alone and isolated and their adult children overburdened with caring for both children and elderly parents.

Families have grown more isolated from each other, yet more dependent on the larger society for their needs. As ties to the outside world have weakened, emotional bonds among family members have intensified. Families frequently hedge their openness to the world around them, seeing the outside world as a hostile or intrusive force from which the family must be protected. A closed family becomes an end in itself, failing in those socializing responsibilities which would modify human self-centeredness and encourage service to the larger society.

With this isolation comes a deep sense of powerlessness and lack of a support system so essential to healthy change. Families resist change because it substantially alters the equilibrium of the family system. Denial of the inevitability of change often precipitates family crisis. Support groups, like Alcoholics Anonymous, have proved how essential support is to successful change. The church, although it talks of community and caring for each other, presently does very little to support families in times of crisis and change. Thus families must generally reach outside the church for support groups.

Studies of which couples are succeeding in marriage show only two measurable factors, the faith life of the couple and their support system. A century ago families thought they had the necessary strength to help individual members and did not need outside help. The individual family unit could depend on its wider extended family for support. Families that had to call for outside help other than in an emergency were considered less good or stable than other families. As the extended family diminished, need for outside support grew.

Many parishes that once provided strong support and care now stress growth, organization, and parish life, neglecting the small caring groups within their structures. The Christian Family Movement (CFM), Teams of Our Lady, and other groups for couples or families flourished in the 1950s, before parish staffs began restructuring the parish. Today, no agency considers the ongoing support of the family as its major task. We have many agencies which offer support to individual family members once the family is in great difficulty. Strangely, we fail to recognize that such structures cannot change individuals while neglecting the family system in which the individual lives.

Sources of Energy and Hope

Waiting for the family gets difficult for parish staff members, who see families caught by changing roles and lifestyle and confused by a new understanding of marriage as a path toward self-fulfillment. Yet church workers easily contribute to this confusion. Many implicitly reaffirm the notion that women's roles are restricted to the home, children, and lesser duties of household life. The church inadvertently supports male abandonment or flight from family obligation through its sense of patriarchy and of the good provider.

Pastoral insensitivity presents a grave obstacle to healthy support of couples. Guidelines so rigidly upheld that they become an excuse to deny Christian marriage or to isolate divorced persons obscure the spirit of Vatican II. Fortunately, parishioners are growing more vocal in their call for pastorally sensitive parish staffs.

The church is blessed by access to its people. In 1988, 73% of American weddings still took place in churches. Two-thirds of Americans are members of churches and a 1993 Gallup Poll showed that 43% go to church at least weekly. Three out of four Catholics say they go to church at least monthly. More than 40% of Catholics say that the church is one of the most important parts of their lives, while another 40% say it is quite important.

Today's Catholics trust their own thinking and experiences more than that of religious leaders. Our growing search for intimacy reflects a new hunger for roots and family bonds. The parish community also needs intimacy, but until we stop avoiding each other for fear of control or of getting hurt we will never listen to each other and share our faith stories and insights openly.

Are there sources of energy which offer hope for improving family ministry? Yes! An active rather than passive laity, who take their baptismal call to discipleship seriously, is finding holiness less in parish life than in the church's daily life in homes and workplaces. As we become more alert to the family-centered church, we will focus more attention on this fundamental unit, convinced that strong families will create a vibrant parish.

Families themselves have much to contribute to these efforts. They can call us away from our attention to the individual, leading us to a greater awareness of relationship-building and intimacy. In our world of independence and autonomy, a sense of the family as an interrelated system reminds us of the futility of ministering pastorally to individuals. In a church which stumbles over social justice awareness, families with a sense of mission teach us greater concern for all our brothers and sisters. For a church long suspicious of experiential knowledge, emphasizing truths learned instead from theologians, families remind us that God is present in and through our unpredicable relationships with one another. Couples who would gladly take on a mentor role for the engaged, newly married, and hurting marriages are the greatest untapped resource for family ministry today.

Minority groups in America, including newer immigrant groups, also offer a source of new energy through their commitment to family. The Jewish sense of a household church shaped the early Christian community and still defines our liturgy. Native Americans remind us the Creator gives all life connectedness, e.g., through women's puberty rites which celebrate the sanctity of the gift of producing new life. Black worship, including prayer and ritual in the family, celebrates with deep emotion such events of life as birth, death, puberty, fertility, harvest, famine, marriage, and tragedy. Hispanic Catholics, rapidly becoming a major segment of the U.S. Catholic Church, have blessed us with counter-cultural values such as devotion to family, gratitude for and love of life, an appreciation for hospitality toward outsiders, and a sense of the sacredness of family meals.

Renewal movements, such as Marriage Encounter, Retrouvaille, and Cursillo, provide a further source of energy in the church today. These peer ministries build on the sharing of personal stories, enabling participants to gain insights into their own experiences while also creating a support system to care for each other. An intense weekend of listening and open sharing provides a conversion experience usually more powerful than that of the R.C.I.A. or preached retreats. Since evangelization happens best in families, how unfortunate that renewal movements do not receive the support they deserve from pastoral staffs.

A church based on rules rather than relationships changes slowly. Family life doesn't work in this legalistic sense. One difficulty with any paradigm making family the primary and central unit of church life lies in how the clergy, who are responsible for church order, can then control family life. In reality, our paradigm must include a shift from control to freedom, trust, and a spontaneous response to God's will. Rather than stress on professed beliefs and rules, emphasis will be on maturity and action as disciples. Family members have minimal religious training and will depend more on experiential learning and peer wisdom. For the parish, this means refocusing energy away from the worship service, which now dominates staff time, to ministries driven more by the needs of members than by institutional planning.

The Portuguese have an axiom: "An ounce of mother is worth a pound of clergy." This likely includes parish staff members. Parish staffs get so caught up in the workload and maintenance of an ailing church that they lose a positive attitude toward the future or lack a vision which can lead to creative action. Persons with a vision see things not as they are but as they ought to be. A vision enables us to put our dreams into action. Such a vision can be created only by leaders who listen to their people and experience the reality surrounding them. A vision must be worth the effort while promising to make a difference. I believe the parish whose vision sees healthy family life as central to its mission will indeed make a difference for families while assuring its future health as well.

Actions to Consider

• Albert Einstein said: "The significant problems we face cannot be solved at the same level of thinking we were at when we created them." The influences in our life, including church and family, have made their silent, unconscious impact on us and help shape our paradigms. Take a look at your paradigms, testing them against reality, with an openness to changing them.

• Think about a paradigm for parish ministry that makes the family and not the parish the central focus, i.e., that focuses on the primary unit of church. Right now, 99% of pastoral staff time is given to gathering the folks for parish events rather than to scattering them for their daily life as church.

• Set up a process for listening to the needs of families. This was central to the Bishops' Pastoral Plan for Family Ministry and makes more certain that the parish meets the needs and interests of parishioners. The needs of members, rather than the ideas of the pastoral staff, should formulate ministry.

• Require parish staff and volunteers to consider what impact any parish events have on the family. The parish competes with families for their time. Every program should be challenged as to whether it strengthens family bonds or contributes to family fragmentation. Recognize that volunteers and staff are also family members.

• Set up a parish family life committee. We did not follow through on early recommendations that parish councils have a family life committee, and few parishes have either such a committee or a family life coordinator to keep the parish focused on the needs of families.

• Call on help from family members to enhance the pastoral message. Most parishioners say they hear little from their parish about marriage and family life. Why not help them remedy this. Invite married couples to help plan homilies, or let committed couples talk on family life. Invite couples to represent family interests on the parish council or committees. The pastoral message needs to acknowledge the strengths and not just decry the failures of family life.

• "The Lord works from the inside out. The world works from the outside in. The world would take people out of the slums. Christ takes the slums out of people, and then they take themselves out of the slums. The world would change men by changing their environment. Christ changes men, who then change their environment. The world would shape human behavior, but Christ can change human nature." (Ezra Taft Benson) Can you apply this to family ministry in the parish?

2

The Journey Together

A family is our first community and most basic way in which the Lord gathers us, forms us and acts in our world. The early church expressed this truth by calling the Christian family a "Domestic Church" or "Church of the Home."

"LOVE NEVER FAILS" (1 COR. 13:8). THE STRESS AND BROKENNESS of family life today make Paul's words seem foolish. While politicians and Christians generally agree on the importance of the family, we are far from achieving a stable environment in which families best grow and function. We face heavy challenges that call not so much for new programs as for a look at our attitudes, values, and our very understanding of family life.

In the early centuries, Christianity began to invert the priorities of Jesus, letting orthodoxy of faith surpass love as the determining mark of the Christian. Persons failing to meet the criteria of faith were rejected and sometimes put to death so that purity of faith might be preserved.

The rules-oriented church in which most of us grew up approached marriage from the legalistic point of view of rights, duties, and contracts. Persons affected by interdenominational marriages, questions of intercommunion, conflicts over birth control or divorce experienced faith not as a living relationship with a loving God, but as rules and dogmas that caused them pain and conflict. Vatican II's vision of the family as a community of life and love and the "school of deeper humanity" gave many hope that attitudes and practices would change.

Over the last three centuries, Western industrialized nations increasingly emphasized the individual over the family.

17

Couples today think it no one else's business whether they marry, how they live their marriage, and whether or not they stay married. Yet family problems and the breakup of marriages affect children, families of origin, neighbors and employers. Family disintegration is the most expensive social problem of our day. As a consequence of individualism, our families easily become an object of blame for our pain rather than our source of strength and support.

The Scientific Paradigm

The family faces disfavor as our scientific world focuses on facts rather than values. Not only is the family linked to values about which we can't argue in meaningful ways, it is linked to controversial and often conservative values. Family values are often thought in conflict with feminist values, with the family judged to be a major source of oppression for women. Some see the essence of family life reflecting the traditional notion of male dominance. In reality, women and family have suffered a similar demeaning and belittling in our technocratic, competitive society. Families and family values still provide the major alternative to a selfish, individualistic mentality. Some hopeful signs of change are evident today, such as fathers spending more time with their children.

We see in our society the beginning of a shift from the scientific paradigm to a new paradigm first formulated in the systems theory. Systems thinking does not deny the importance of the individual parts of the system, rather it stresses the relationship of the parts and how they work together in a system as most important.

An individual plays various roles in his or her family. When particular ministries or services of the church help an individual, this causes changes in how he or she relates to the family as a whole and to individual members. The family must adjust to changes in the individual, which may introduce conflict and tension within the family as it adjusts to the changed member. It might consciously or unconsciously exert pressure on the individual to resume his or her former roles, behaviors and values. It may reject the individual. The family may struggle to live with the tensions the changes create, which then causes changes within the family system and in the individual members of the family. Such family dynamics are triggered when a member participates in an intensive weekend experience such as Marriage Encounter or Cursillo, enters into the conversion process of R.C.I.A., joins an A.A. program or makes other major changes.

A family perspective that embraces the systems theory can help us understand how ministries and programs for the individual affect his or her family life and how the family's response affects the reception of ministries by the individual. A family perspective seeks to bridge potential conflict and provide support to both the individual and the family in coping with the changes that have been initiated by the church ministries.

Church ministries have generally been oriented toward the radical individualism that permeates our culture. If there is a need, we simply add another program for youth, for parents, for the separated and divorced. Such ministries do not respond to families as a unit in appropriate ways. Ministry to families is not just another ministry added to the others, but an awareness of how all ministry impacts the family as a system within the larger systems of the church and society. John Paul II reminds us in *Familiaris Consortio* that no plan of pastoral action at any level of the church should ever be undertaken without first understanding its potential impact on families (FC, 70).

The dilemma today is not the moral decay of the family but the spiritual emptiness of our culture. The family is often the place where the crisis of faith occurs. This makes it the primary place where the healing of our culture's spiritual emptiness must begin.

Since the heart of culture is some form of spirituality, our cultural struggle is fundamentally a spiritual struggle. A rapid process of change, fueled by revolutions in science and human behavior, placed us in the midst of a new era for families. The family grew rather powerless in the face of powerful social forces, and now struggles to survive and adapt. On the one hand, the family seems to be caught in a crisis of confidence, reacting angrily to forces of change such as new lifestyles, working mothers, rising divorce rates, and the influence of the media. Government programs often work against the family through biased welfare policies and heavy taxation of the poor. Yet we devote a lot of attention to forming new patterns of intimacy.

Political parties in America use the image of support for the family while refusing to take a vigorous stand. Liberals and conservatives both proclaim the centrality of the family in society, but differ on the policy implications.

Persons with liberal views look at society as a collection of individuals bound together by voluntary contracts or covenants.

Husband-wife and even parent-child relationships are viewed as contracts. Justice and peace movements stress the rights of individuals, such as women's rights and civil rights, but are generally silent on family life. They tend to forget the spiritual source for their justice stands, advocating religious privacy with regard to moral matters. This creates such ironies as pro-life advocates sometimes voting against family bills while supporting the rights of the unborn.

Conservative movements insist on the fundamental principle of family life as the basis of society, but often exist in defense of patriarchy, sexism, and a radical oppression of the human experience. Conservatives warn us about the crisis of secular values, yet they would recover the threatened spiritual foundation of our traditional culture by authority and control. The right often attempts to recover a nostalgic past through a return to the patriarchal family and a traditional image of God as a male judge totally above creation.

Liberals desire greater government activism, judging social conservatives as nostalgic for an unreal image of the nuclear family and moral absolutists who stigmatize those who do not fit into their traditional family model. Conservatives decry the permissiveness of the liberal ethic, which they claim has promoted a culture of hedonistic individualism directly opposed to family life and rooted in a moral relativism which insists that all lifestyles are morally and socially equal.

Since the Reformation, the Catholic model has been religious professionals who rejected family life and ordinary human labor for the sake of apostolic work. This fostered a top down theology that held experiential knowledge suspect, especially the experience of families. Today John Paul II calls upon the church to develop a lay-centered spirituality centered in work, the family, and culture. Both the left and the right struggle with this changing model. The liberal left, with their theological reflection, publishing firms, justice and peace centers, and retreat houses reflects the view of the apostolic, professional church. They tend to exclude lay energy from their core. The conservative and reactionary new movements embody much more the lay-centered, family-centered vision of the church. They consciously seek a spirituality that embodies family and home rituals, supports the role of marriage and parenting, and stresses responsibility in the family, while often reaffirming an authoritarian, patriarchal understanding of the church, family, and social traditions. Thus the behavior of the right and left is opposite of their ideology. The religious left forgets that in tradition and its institutions, like family and church, we also meet God. One of my priest friends, a well-known justice fighter, had a conversion experience while taking part in a Marriage Encounter. There he realized that many justice advocates are harsh and lacking in love. We most often discover God's presence in the reality of loving family relationships. This is why bodily experiences, such as sexuality, take on such moral proportions. Our body is our first religious encounter with the Mystery expressed in creation.

Modern thinking has tried to end the sexual discrimination against women by casting them into a male social role. In the face of an anti-family culture, we need to recover the female symbol as cherisher of life. The modern attempt of males to crush nature and the feminine, e.g., by mass technological abortion and control of fertility, is in essence a rejection of partnership in the process of reproduction. We need to heal men in a new shared model of marriage based not on patriarchy but on partnership, where spousal love can flourish even more.

The Catholic Voice

It is a fundamental premise in the Catholic community that our family is central to our development as a full person and our becoming and remaining a Christian. John Paul II reminds us that "As the family goes, so goes the world." He might readily add ". . . and so goes the church." The family is the first and vital cell of all societies, social and ecclesial. The very core of the Church is linked to the well-being of the family, and the future of the Church passes through the family (*Familiaris Consortio* 3, 75).

In preparation for the Synod on the Laity in 1987, U.S. bishops asked American Catholics where they most find God in their lives. Most said they found God in their marriage and family life. The bishops then asked people where they most needed help from the Church, and the overwhelming response was "in my marriage and family life."

The bishops had earlier acknowledged this need in their *Pastoral Plan for Family Ministry* in 1978. When the bishops then went on to write their pastorals on peace and on the economy rather than lead the U.S. church's efforts at family ministry in the 1980s, families continued to suffer. While the bishops recommitted to this plan for the decade of the 1990s, their commitment may well be reflected in budget reductions and closings of many family life offices.

Vatican II spoke of the "domestic church." I prefer the term "family-centered church." New Testament and patristic understanding of this term suggests the Christian family is church precisely because the important dimensions of the whole church can be identified there. While the Fathers, guided by Ephesians 5:32, continued to see profound bonds between ecclesiastical and conjugal communities, church leaders seem to dismiss the family-centered church by saying that the term lacks ecclesiological precision. Families, on the other hand, intuitively realize their faith makes little sense apart from what goes on in their daily experience of family relationships.

Although they may not be able to describe what it means to be a sacrament, most families have moments when they realize they are in the presence of a Mystery greater than themselves. These may be such moments as discovering a first pregnancy, childbirth, an intimate sexual experience, or reconciliation after a painful misunderstanding. Perhaps the most difficult truth to believe over the course of our lifetime is that we are important enough to be loved by God. Nothing makes this more credible than our discovery of being important to and loved by another person.

What a profound revelation to recognize one's family as church, as people in a relationship of committed love with God and with one another. For a Christian family, being church is both vocation and identity. The family-centered church is God's plan for the family. A couple's and family's sense of worth comes from the One who called them to belong to each other. Too often God's plan is ineffective because families either do not understand this call or have no idea of how to live their vocation. Families easily become isolated units serving their personal needs rather than living a sense of mission.

Although we tend to think of marriage and family life as something very ordinary, it is not ordinary to God, who calls families to be a powerful sign as a community of love. One of the most serious problems facing families is the lack of quality time together. Such time is necessary if families are to be church, i.e., genuine communities of faith and love. Members are often more committed to their careers, hobbies, athletics or other people than to their spouse, children, parents or siblings. To fulfill God's command to love each other, thus choosing the Lord as first priority, is not a one-time decision but a continual choice.

Spouses need help to recognize their vocation to be a family-centered church. Everything else they do flows from that foundational calling. It is precisely in loving a husband or wife "as Christ loved the church" (Eph. 5:25) and parenting children as God parents (Eph. 6:4, Col. 3:21) that a person learns how to serve in the broader church. Any service beyond themselves is an extension of the demonstrated service and love within the family-centered church. The Christian family is ministry, the first and foundational ministry for God's people. Restoring this dynamic vision of the family-centered church could be the very seed that renews the contemporary church and eventually transforms our secularized culture.

This really requires a fresh new way of thinking for both pastoral staffs and families. New and novel programs will not accomplish this. No mere human stategy will rebuild the

Christian family. Husbands and wives need to understand that God's plan is for them to begin where they are called, in the family and not in the local parish or out doing public service. God called them to first minister to their families.

It's time we look again to the New Testament and the apostolic age to rediscover an important truth about the structure of the church. Structure grew out of the need and experience of the people. When the earliest Christians were banned from the synagogue, they naturally gathered first in private homes (Acts 2:46) and then in larger groups. Family was the first church, then a structured family of families emerged. We need to return to the original vision, renewing our sense of the Christian family before we can rebuild our understanding of the larger Christian church. Rather than just living in the world as families who happen to be Christian, families are called to be and live as the family centered church, the living stones spoken of by Peter (1 Peter 2:5).

The conviction that the family is the most basic religious community predates the Gospel. In Jewish tradition the home, not the synagogue, is the center of religious life. Jesus defined the New Testament description of the family as church: "Where two or three are gathered in my name, there am I in their midst" (Mt. 18:20). Whatever else these words describe, they clearly apply to the family. By the fourth century, St. John Chrysostom was writing of the family as "ecclesia." It is significant that the fathers at Vatican II decided to discuss the family in the document on the church, not in a separate document.

Even though the scriptures relate the holiness of God's plan for family life, the church gradually began to adopt a popular philosophy that divided reality into the holy and the unholy, the sacred and the secular, the spiritual and the material. The spiritual was holy, as when people went off to the desert as hermits or to the monastery to pray. Material objects were unholy. The division of body and soul regarded the body and sex as material and therefore evil, while praising abstinence as holier than married sexuality. Eventually, celibacy was considered a strength and marriage a weakness. Marriage became a second rate vocation rather than a way of living in God's own image (Gen. 1:27-28). Christians then escaped from their homes and daily lives to find God in church. Clergy focused on the personal salvation of Christians rather than on their daily living in the world.

The church's theology has often had a negative impact on families. Following the Reformation and the Council of Trent, church leaders intentionally made the parish the normative model for religious participation to eliminate certain abuses which might come through religious associations or family groups. To accomplish this, they increasingly emphasized issues of faith, salvation, sin and the sacraments as the domain of the individual. Unintentionally, subsequent theology did not place enough emphasis on the role of the family and its importance in the development and maintenance of faith, nor the familial and social consequences of sin.

Vatican II tried to recapture the early Church's understanding of family, defining it again as church by its mission and its special aptitude for transmitting the Gospel. After the Council, Paul VI frequently called the family the domestic church or "little church," the most basic cell not only of society but of the church as well.

In his homily opening the 1980 Synod on the Family, Pope John Paul II said the family is meant to "constitute the church in its fundamental dimension." In *Familiaris Consortio,* following the Synod, the pope urged that pastoral care for the family be treated as a real priority. He linked the very core of the church to the well-being of the family, noting that the future of the church passes through the family (FC 75).

Several recent church statements hold added significance for family ministry. The *New Code of Canon Law,* promulgated in the 1980s, acknowledged the family unit. Parents and families are seen as another structure beyond the parish, not solely as recipients of ministry or responsible for members' participation in church life. The family has a fundamental role as an agent of ministry in Christian formation and service parallel to the role of the parish and in partnership with it. To perform this mission and service is itself a ministry of the church.

In 1989, the U.S. Bishops issued *Putting Children and Families First: A Challenge for Our Church, Nation and World,* calling for a reinvigorated pastoral ministry to families. In their subsequent action plan to implement this statement, they gave attention primarily to programs for children, who easily become victims of family disintegration, rather than to efforts to strengthen family life and prevent family breakdown. If we can believe the statistic that 90% of those in U.S. jails are from broken homes, should our first priority be to help victims of family breakdown or to prevent families from breaking down in the first place?

Our current ministry does not seem to be changing the plight of the American family. The obvious answer is not more programs, staff, or budget but a different approach. Emphasis on a family perspective in all our ministries should help. Ministries of the church, even those to individuals, touch the very fiber and life of the family. Within the church, we have looked at ministry much more from the perspective of the "parish family."

Somehow, our paradigm shifted from the New Testament household-centered church to a parish-centered church. Where in the New Testament can one find any mention of parish? Prior to Vatican II, a number of parallel organizations existed, such as the Christian Family Movement, Young Christian Workers, and Catholic Physicians' Guilds. These organizations were often centers of energy for their members and for the greater church. Catholic life after Vatican II became more parish-centered, with renewed liturgies, RCIA, parish-centered religious education, parish councils, Renew, Parish Renewal Weekends, and lay ministries. This narrowed focus neglected the family and even concern for the larger society.

A paradigm that views the parish as the central unit of church creates a barrier to family ministry. We then began to navel gaze on what happens in the parish buildings rather than on what happens where the church lives all week long in our homes, factories, schools and public offices. Concentrating our attention on parish life, we wonder why our efforts bear so little fruit. The family and parish are interdependent. A paradigm shift which acknowledges the family as the basic unit of church also reminds us that the parish will be as strong as the families that comprise it. Our parishes languish today because they are made up largely of families who are being evangelized and influenced far more effectively by a secular culture than by the church. When families take their mission seriously, being church in their homes and in the marketplace, the church will be alive and vibrant in our parishes, and church buildings will ring with joy and praise of the Lord.

Mitch Finley quotes a pastor who said: "The parish is either a family of families or it is a whole bunch of people going through the motions once a week."* Until parish leaders nourish every dimension of Christian family life, parishes will flounder. Until the family-centered church re-emerges, the parish will remain a sacramental service station.

Achieving a Family Perspective

While a family focus does not eliminate the need for perspective on the individual, the small groups of which we are members, and society as a whole, it places a deliberate focus on the primary community to which most people belong, the family. We live in a series of relationships, not in isolation. Family relationships are among the most important for any person. We need a strong perspective on the family, because our society is pro-individual and pro-institutional, a result of the scientific paradigm.

Institutions that were originally created to support families validate the family functions of intimacy and mutual support while subtly suggesting they can perform other functions such as education, health care, recreation, and religious formation better than families can. E.g., family members are often viewed as a hindrance to healing the sick, apparent in limited visiting hours and exclusion of children from hospitals.

In reality, the family is a stronger agent of educational success than the school, the primary health care provider, and the basic teacher of religious values. Father Andrew Greeley adds: "The family is a more important institution of religious socialization than the church." Most Americans agree they learned their core values in the home.

Institutions, whether school, hospital, or parish, can empower or disempower families. They properly view their role as one of partnership with and support for families. Those

---

* Mitch Finley, "A Family Ecclesiology," *America*, Vol. 149 (July 30, 1983), p. 50.

who attempt to help a troubled individual, such as an alcoholic or a depressed person, are much less likely to succeed if they do not at some level also work with that individual's immediate family. This seems especially true of spouses in a troubled marriage.

A family perspective recognizes that church ministries, though often designed for the individual, affect families through their entire life cycle. Ministries, in turn, are also affected by the individual's family, which influences the benefits the individual receives, either accepting any conversion and change or resisting and ultimately shutting down the individual's new found excitment.

A family perspective means that parish staffs attempt to empower families and support them in fulfilling their own functions rather than replacing them. To do this, we first need to listen to families and become sensitive to how ministries impact on them. How has shifting religious education to the professionals taken the formation of religious values out of the home? How can the home and the parish work together in sacramental formation or moral development?

Many parish activities are traditionally and properly segregated by sex, age, and status. This practice has its negative effects on building family relationships. Do we alienate generations from one another and promote society's tendency toward age segregation? Are singles isolated from the life of the parish? Do we discourage networks of families from forming in the parish unless parish leaders are involved? Even when the nature of parish activities necessarily segregate people we can maintain a family dimension. Senior citizens' activities can bring together extended families. Schedulers of lay ministry can make certain that Dad, Mom and their children all assist at the same liturgy.

By far the most vital service a parish can provide for its families is genuine affirmation and support for the central and irreplaceable role that the family-centered church plays in Christian spiritual formation. A congregation that truly comprehends the central mission of family life within its body will significantly alter the approach to family ministry. Dolores Leckey maintains that the family-centered church has much to teach the gathered church about what it means to live together creatively and faithfully. Even if broken, families are loved and blessed by God and given gifts to fulfill their vocation.

The challenge for the parish community is to lift up what society no longer provides, a vision of marriage and family as a place of holiness, beauty, and spiritual vitality, through preaching, teaching, and programming. As recently as the 1960s, we had an overarching belief that family life was important. Lacking that compelling conviction today, families are like lone rangers trying to live their call without much community support. By reminding the family of its graced task and supporting its essential vocation, the church sets the family free for mission instead of using up family resources for institutional maintenance.

Religious leaders find it difficult to set before us any clear ideal of the family because it might seem too much like condemning those who do not meet it. We often say too little about the family because we are unable to articulate what it should be at its best. We sometimes say too much because we do not take seriously enough the ways in which the family is central to God's plan.

The family is the sphere in which God is at work in us, shaping and molding us to be a people who genuinely share God's life of love. If the church has a distinctive insight to offer, it may be that the family is a community that ought to transmit a way of life. Spouses, parents, and children learn what it means to love unconditionally, and to be grateful recipients of a love to which they have no rightful claim. Families may fall short of this ideal but most come closer than we think. Americans still place family among their most enduring values. They need a word that interprets the bond between spouses and between parents and children in light of God's plan and gives us all a renewed sense of what it means to live within a family.

Contrary to popular belief, the best marriages and happiest families don't happen because people concentrate, first of all, on the unity of their relationship but when a couple and the family as a whole expend their energies on something bigger than themselves. Chris and Mary Ann learned this: "We have something to say about the sacrament of marriage. When we were first married, everybody told us to just spend the time on ourselves. That was a lonely hell. We were lucky, because we made a Marriage Encounter weekend when we were married only one year. There the message was to share our lives with others. That has made all the difference."

Jesus' model for ministry was footwashing. Mary, the sister of Lazarus and Martha, prepared Jesus for his death by washing and anointing him on his way to Jerusalem to die. Jesus repeated this ritual by washing the feet of his apostles, an act of one who served. Loving them with an act of service, or serving them with an act of love, Jesus asked them to do the same. The call to ministry is a call to serve one another in love.

Family ministry is based on certain assumptions. One is that all families, no matter how hurting or fragmented, have tremendous strengths and power to help and support other families. Another is that individuals and families who have been through a certain experience have a quality of caring and support to offer others in a similar situation that is unique and healing.

From this concept follows the principle of like to like ministry. The real experts in marriage and family ministry are spouses and family members. There are times when specialized, professional help is needed, but the basic ministry to families lies in the day to day support that family members and peers give to each other at the death of a parent or child, with questions about parenting, or during family and marital difficulties.

Married couples experience vulnerability and need for support and nurturing. Wanda and Terry, as peer ministers to hurting couples, share their own story: "We went to three marriage counselors and a priest for help with our marriage. Each one told us that our problem was communication, yet no one helped us learn how to communicate. Instead, they all suggested we separate. We didn't want to separate, and we already knew we couldn't communicate, but couldn't learn how on our own."

Henri Nouwen adds insight into ministry. "Ministers are men and women without power who live in the name of the Lord and often see him when they least expect it."[*]

Ministers are powerless. Power keeps others in our control. Struggles to control each other are often part of the dynamic of ministry. Family ministers are not there to control or to change others; rather, they share vulnerability as they relate their own stories with a deep compassion and caring for other families. Real powerlessness exists in our honesty and sincerity.

Ministers are powerless, but they live in the name of the Lord. Living in Jesus' name points to an affectionate, intimately personal relationship. If ministry can bear fruit only with, in, and through Jesus Christ, then persons who do family ministry must be concerned for an ongoing communion with the Lord who called them to this ministry. Without prayer, ministry quickly deteriorates into a busy life in which our own needs for acceptance and affection start to dominate our actions, and being busy becomes a way of convincing ourselves of our own importance.

Ministers are powerless people who live in the name of the Lord and are seers of God. We see God wherever people are in need and cry out for our help. Family ministers have gained their own awareness of God, often through their personal struggles, and can now point to God's presence when pain blinds hurting families to anything beyond their own problems. Tom and Vivien reflect this reality:

> We have certainly received more for our own relationship than we have ever given. Yet through the years and the hundreds of couples we have presented weekends to we never cease to be awed, humbled and amazed at the healing and beauty that God's love can bring out of so much hurt and pain. You just realize you know there was no way that whatever you said could have brought about that much change in anyone. You know the healing power of Jesus' love is present and active through the power of prayer.[*]

John Paul II reminds us: "The modern Christian family is often tempted to be discouraged and distressed at the growth

---

[**]   Henri Nouwen, "The Monk and the Cripple: Toward a Spirituality for Ministry," *America*, (March 15, 1980), pp. 205-210.
[*]   Vol. 5, No. 1 (February, 1988), p. 13.

of its difficulties; it is an eminent form of love to give it back its reasons for confidence in itself, in the riches it possesses by nature and grace, and in the mission which God has entrusted to it" (FC, 86).

Actions to Consider

• A theology of family life is developing, based largely on experiences of couples and families. Pastoral staffs would do well to read some of the developing theology, e.g., the writings of Mitch Finley. Groups of laity can also do some theologizing based on their experiences. The Christian Family Movement's OBSERVE, JUDGE, ACT form a good basis for searching and questioning, necessary elements in the process of growth toward mature faith.

• Affirm the ministry that happens in families. Where do we find better models for Jesus' footwashing ministry than in moms washing babies' bottoms and family laundry, dads struggling with budget shortages and listening patiently to teenagers who color their hair orange to get attention, or spouses caring for sick partners? People get all excited about lay ministry in their parish without recognizing the important ministry they perform daily in the family-centered church.

• The U.S. bishops have made some good statements on family life, even though we are not quick to develop such ministry. Distribute copies of *Follow the Way of Love* to parish members (it's quite readable) and use this material with discussion groups.

• Dare to speak with authority about family matters. For example, society has seen fathers as incidental while scripture affirms the importance of the male role. Today we hear about the "father wound" which causes difficulties for so many youngsters because their father is absent or uninvolved. The average father spends three and one half minutes per week face to face with his child, according to one study. Challenge the men of the parish to become better fathers.

• Evaluate all ministry programs in the parish in terms of a family perspective to see how they contribute to or fail to contribute to family life. The church has not escaped the individualism that so marks our society today. Ascetical theology was individual centered, based on saving the individual's soul, rather than relationship oriented or aware of family systems. Family spirituality will be very cognizant of family systems and how anything that affects one member of the family affects all the members.

• Go back to look at your parish mission statement. Does it have family as the end in mind? The mission statement is comprised of our most basic paradigms and reflects our vision and values. A mission statement in which members have participated creates unity and guidelines for action.

3

A House Built on Rock

> We honor all families who, in the face of obstacles,
> remain faithful to Christ's way of love. The church
> of the home can live and grow in every family.

MANY QUESTION IF "FAMILY-CENTERED CHURCH" ISN'T AN OXYMO-
ron. Beyond a doubt, pastoral leaders need to rethink those
paradigms which shape their action regarding marriage, family life and divorce. The church model for family life is
usually the nuclear and extended family of Dad, Mom, and
several children, who are closely tied to the grandparents and
other relatives and friends who provide a support system. In
reality, families are much more diverse, are scarred by problems and worries, and marked by frequent failure, with much
need for reconciliation and outside support. Thus our definition of the American family must be much broader than the
nuclear family, embracing the diversity of American families
and recognizing that God's own life can be touched in single-
parent families, elderly couples, and all the other units that
make up the American family.

This variety of family lifestyles has to move our ministry
beyond programs for such target groups as the engaged or
hurting marriages to a concern for the whole of family life.
Like Cardinal Bernadin's seamless garment approach to the
sanctity of life, we need a perspective that embraces and supports the whole of family life. Couples and families do not
merely need help at pivotal times in their life, as beneficial as
these programs may be, but an ongoing support and enrichment.

Nor does viewing marriage as a contract provide an adequate understanding of marriage. If we accept Avery Dulles'
model of the church as a community of disciples, how does

this fit the smallest unit of the church, the family? Have we not approached marriage primarily from the legalistic point of view, noting that the wedding be properly conducted, that the marriage be consumated, that the couple be open to children, etc.? Sacrament, however, implies a living relationship with God, not merely fulfilling certain conditions to receive grace from God.

Disciples are called by God. This free, personal call does not come from the church, but from Jesus, the focal point of the Christian's life. The vocation to discipleship means a radical break from the values of this world to embrace the values of the kingdom. Disciples are called together as a community, seek unity through their love for one another, and are then sent forth into the world for ministry and mission. Marriage means commitment of a man and a woman to the joint venture of discipleship together, aware that Jesus promises to be present where two or three gather as Christians. As parents, they will be responsible for the primary socialization of new members of the community.

We still face the complex task of appraising the Vatican II vision of the family as truly church. In this, we rely on the experience of married couples and families as much as on the theologians. Where do they find God in their lives? What in the experience of these intimate relationships is holy? What they reveal forces us to rethink our theology. Our thinking is incomplete if it does not refer back to the lived experiences of God's people. How we interpret these experiences can give us new insight and direction.

The dualism which shaped the pre-Vatican II church viewed marriage as a lesser vocation and made sexuality part of the material world as opposed to the spiritual. Women were considered less than men, which fostered patriarchy. Celibacy was superior to marital sexuality. The sacrament was conferred on the relationship from outside rather than flowing from the love relationship of the spouses. The institutional church set rules for marriage and did not view family members as potential ministers.

Daily life in the family helps us understand the meaning of marriage as sacrament, e.g., how much of our spirituality is rooted in our bodies. While the church too often distinquished between body and spirit, the experience of married couples says we cannot separate the two. As we experience our love for each other in everyday ways, we know the love God has for us. We are called to be grace for each other. We learn that God can be trusted to renew and heal our love each day, even when the going gets difficult. As our love for each other draws us into intimacy, we learn the meaning of John's words: ". . . if we love one another, God remains in us, and [God's] love is brought to perfection in us" (1 John 4:12).

Becoming Married

Apart from the wedding ceremony, most engaged and newly married couples would scarcely sense they are important to the church. Moved by escalating divorce rates after mid-century, Catholic leaders initiated marriage preparation programs to make certain marriages would last. An advertisement several years ago said: "If you don't know what to give couples getting married, why not give them divorce insurance?" Then, it implied, if the marriage doesn't last, they will have something to fall back on. We could provide much better "divorce insurance" through good preparation programs, premarital counseling rigorous enough to help couples with weak relationships discover this before marriage, and mentor couples who share values and not just information. The church would then move beyond the wedding business to prepare couples for lifelong marriages.

Enthusiasm for marriage preparation has already peaked and waned. Reflecting on their experiences, married couples in the 1960s challenged the church to do more for couples preparing for marriage. New programs, like Catholic Engaged Encounter, were unique as they involved the laity in this ministry. At the Call to Action in Detroit in 1976, many lay delegates wanted a statement calling the church to prepare couples for marriage "with the same seriousness with which we prepare young men for the priesthood."

Today, despite growing brokenness among young adults approaching the church for marriage, enthusiasm has given way to preparation programs that easily become rigid and inflexible. Failing to hear a compelling message about marriage from the church, many engaged persons approach marriage preparation indifferently or reluctantly. A study of one diocese in the early 1990s indicated that only two out of every ten engaged couples participated in a formal marriage preparation program. More comprehensive programs are being replaced by one day pre-Cana sessions or four hours of video instruction. Such short programs convey a powerful message to the engaged about the importance or lack of importance assigned to their sacrament by the church.

Frequently not active church participants, young adults get very little sacramental and spiritual input. If they grew up in unhealthy family backgrounds, they get almost no help to look at how their parents' behavior imprinted on their relationship skills. If these marriages fail, we deal much more seriously with spouses when they approach the church for an annulment. Tribunals generally have larger staffs than family life offices.

Engaged couples want help to survive in marriage. They may, however, experience the church as more concerned about fidelity to church rules and sexual morality than about their vocation. The moment of falling in love and making a commitment to marry provides the most powerful moment for evangelization in the life of most Catholics. At this time, persons must confront the wrenching question of whether or not they are lovable enough for someone to commit a lifetime to them. When we experience another's total love, we frequently also discover God's unconditional love for us.

Policies will never do for the engaged what living witnesses of marital commitment can do. Paul and Rita can testify to this. Spotting a couple in the supermarket who had been on the first Catholic Engaged Encounter weekend they presented eleven years earlier, Paul and Rita invited the couple to their home to talk about this experience. They could hardly believe what they heard as this couple quoted from the team sharings on that weekend and related how they lived these values in their marriage. A University of California study affirmed that Catholic Engaged Encounter brought "a change of values that will last a lifetime." How many couples, however, get even one weekend of preparation?

Although many parishes now have their own programs, few are outstanding. Convenience seems to be replacing quality. Presentors share a spirituality too often removed from daily life rather than a lived spirituality of matching socks, asking forgiveness, and hanging in there with each other. It's easier to give advice to passive listeners than to help a couple communicate deeply about such complex issues as religious differences, family backgrounds, values and expectations. Actually, marriage preparation starts in our homes. Dual careers, dysfunctional families, the high divorce rate, television and other activities which divide the family and limit communication dimish the effectiveness of today's family as preparer for marriage. Many children from unhealthy families lose their true self, develop self-protective survival behaviors, and pull away often from adult relationships because of a poor self-image. When difficulties occur in their marriages, they find family and friends more ready to encourage them to separate than to reconcile and work through the difficulties.

How do we counteract the message society reflects to the engaged by all the teasing, manipulative advice, and focus on fancy weddings? Individualism motivates persons to marry for self-gain, a "What's in it for me?" attitude, where spouses come together like two empty buckets seeking to be filled. Who is going to do the filling? Such relationships become life-draining rather than life-giving. Real love, in contrast, asks "Who can I be for you?" Who talks to the engaged about the distinctively Christian message that "love is not self-seeking" (1 Cor. 13:5)?

Don't blame the engaged. Despite media messages promising pleasure without responsibility and hinting that most couples experience infidelity and divorce, couples do want a lifelong marriage. My experience suggests most would choose a good marriage preparation program if encouraged. When marriage preparation represents a task for many ministers, lay and cleric, engaged couples rightly expect more.

Do we neglect the engaged primarily because this age group questions faith issues and frequently fails to attend church? What then, about the neglect felt by young marrieds and by the parents of those preparing for marriage? A professional man told a U.S. bishops' hearing: "The hardest job I have ever had as an adult is raising my children. And I can say – without blame but with intended objectivity – that the church has been of very little help."

We readily say that a couple "got married" on the day of their wedding. Yet a lot of becoming married happens in the early years after the wedding. In today's fast-moving society, newly marrieds feel a lot of stress if they try to reconcile traditional religious values with the contemporary message to grab all they can out of life. Reconciliation of faith with lifestyle among the young married couples is critical for the future of the church. A high percentage of these couples are leaving or have left the church, which seems to abandon them after the wedding rather than support them through a very difficult time of adjustment. Some will return, others won't.

What can we do to help young couples remain a part of the faith community? At first glance, it seems they don't have time or interest for parish life. Most are not involved with church activities, yet they consider themselves spiritual. They are in the process of major life transitions, breaking away from their families of origin, exerting a new found independence, starting new careers, becoming adult and responsible. Unlike the engaged, who think they know everything about their partner, newly marrieds are frequently baffled and ready for help from a friend or relative.

Expending all their energy on trying to find out who they are and what they want to be, young marrieds' relationship to a church doesn't fit well into all this frenzied self-discovery. It did momentarily when they asked to be married in the church, but that church seemed far more concerned that they meet church requirements than in helping them grow into a sacrament.

Parish staffs today walk the difficult tightrope between pastoral response and official teaching. If young marrieds can be welcomed into the church with and in spite of their issues and opinions, their future children are also being welcomed and the church community grows. If they are alienated from the church, they are often lost to the church community forever.

There are many reasons why young married couples stay away from the church. Many have not had a positive experience of church and disconnect themselves from it. Statistically, youth generally make the decision whether or not to participate in church life at age 12 or 13, so many have been disconnected for a long time. Many young adults don't agree with what they hear the hierarchical church saying. Some believe that if they cannot buy into the church's views on birth control, abortion, or interfaith practices, they shouldn't become involved at all. Youth are generally distrustful of institutions, especially one that seems to offer little where they are at. Many grew up angry at the church because they watched their parents endure the pain of a divorce or an insensitive priest.

Many who left will return as expectant parents or parents of young children. They feel they still have a right to what the church offers its baptized members. They need a welcoming community to receive them back with open arms, as the prodigal father welcomed his son. Young families usually come searching for something they feel is missing in their lives. They may be looking for a community with similar values, a chance to give their children a faith tradition, simply wanting baptism for their child, pressured by relatives to have their child baptized, or motivated by a decision as a couple to return to active practice of their faith.

The highest divorce rate occurs in the first three years of marriage, when the efforts to build a relationship intensify. In previous times the extended family or friendly neighbors provided a support and understanding that most young marrieds lack today. Couples need peer support and an atmosphere where common concerns can be shared. Opportunities can be built around pre-baptismal programs, parenting skills groups, or sponsor couples on a one-to-one basis.

Once we get young couples back to the church through marriage preparation or baptism of a child, we need to help them stay connected by building relationships with them, offering what they need, and getting them involved. How we offer the church to them and the way we accept them and form relationships with them is key. If we are respectful of their relationship and the place where they are on their journey as Christians, we allow the Spirit to work in them. As open, authentic, and accepting Christians, our example speaks more powerfully to young couples than any of our words ever could. We witness in this way to God's love for us and to our love for each other.

The church is basically about a people striving to see God. That means the more churched members do not have all the answers, but also seek to find the holy in their lives by being vulnerable and reflective about their experiences. For years, however, pastoral leaders have focused on programs that teach doctrine, expecting people would then find effective ways to relate faith to their daily lives.

A graph showing the physical and faith development of a person hints at why childhood education in not enough. We grow rapidly after birth and reach physical maturity at about age 24. Faith development does not look much different at 24 than it does at six. After thirty, our faith grows significantly and after fifty it skyrockets. Thus, faith is not simply the knowledge about God we learn as children or adults. It is a relationship that grows as we experience the movement of God in such key moments of our life as falling in love, having a baby, or losing a parent. We are born into a spiritual relationship through the frustrations, tears, joys, celebrations, laughter, feelings, and experiences of daily life.

Strangely, we deem it foolish to undertake careers or do business without adequate preparation, yet enter into marriage with little preparation. In the romance stage, we expect marriage to somehow have a magical effect if we marry in the church. Love, we presume, will overcome all obstacles. Marriage preparation programs need to help couples in the romance stage face reality and the demands of relationship building. Then we need to support them in their decision to love through the disillusionment and misery stages of early marriage.

Enriching Marriage and Family

The church generally neglects the already married couple. Parishes do not have a strategy to strengthen the marriages of their members. Should this not be at the heart of the pastoral mission, especially when marital breakup devastates so many members?

I think that marriage is successful as long as both spouses keep on trying to learn to be married well," says Kathy Finley. "When it comes to marriage, success isn't arriving at a destination, success is the journey itself."*

When a couple begin their marital journey together, they are scarcely prepared to become parents. The roles of mother or father, disciplinarian, teacher, doctor, chauffeur, referee, nutritionist, and counselor lie beyond their experience and preparation. In order to successfully fulfill all the roles that parents must play, couples need to look beyond themselves for support and assistance. Most of this support will come not from the parish but from couples supporting each other through the challenges parents face today.

Mothers who work outside the home, for example, hurry to get their children dressed, fed and off to school or to the child-care center so they can get to work. After work they race home in the traffic to pick their children up, make dinner, do the laundry and dishes, bathe and find time for the children, help with homework, and so much more. They need emotional and spiritual support. Such support becomes even more essential when families go through a job loss, illness of a family member, or a difficult pregnancy. Support from other families who help with a meal, child care, and encouragment at these times says someone cares. Parish staffs, meanwhile, need to recognize how little time these folks have for any program.

Raising a family is also a life-long learning process, as children go through infancy, preschool, puberty, adolescence, young adulthood, the beginning of marriage and parenting. Each phase brings new challenges, rewards, joys and sorrows. Parents need to prioritize time and to know where to reach out for support when crises occur.

Parish staff easily overlook the fact that daily life can be an overwhelming task for the family centered church. How we help parents find time away for a day of recollection, a marriage enrichment evening, support groups, family gather-

---

* *St. Anthony Messenger,* (February, 1991), p. 30.

ings, or aid during a family crisis, is equally as significant as liturgies relevant to family life. We must be willing to accept families where they are and to listen carefully to their needs, realizing that healthy parishes depend on the strength of families. Placing guilt trips on families for not participating more in parish events is counterproductive.

A century ago families saw themselves as a unit able to help individual members. The twentieth-century family depends upon many other groups for survival. Without the extended family, however, individual households are now forced to rely more than ever on their own emotional resources. Outside influences, from two career families to the value system espoused by television programs to the structure of public education and specialized health care, all impact on the family.

Agencies that verbally support family life tend to foster separateness and survival of the fittest. Most of our structures support individual family members, e.g., public schools, social work agencies, and mental health programs. We fail to see that such structures cannot change the individual without changing the family system in which the individual lives. Family systems are very resistant to change. Members habituated to the status quo will try to undermine change, e.g., by placing the blame for family difficulties on one person.

The church is the only agency in our society that has all the members of the family as its clientele, reaching persons through the complete life cycle from birth to death. Yet the energy of the Christian Family Movement in the 1950s and Marriage Encounter in the 1980s has given way to the frustrating task of helping families survive in a fast and hostile world. Enrichment is based on an assumption that families already possess strengths that can be developed and that change and growth are positive goals. The first obstacle might be the dangerous belief that religious persons and healthy families do not have problems. In fact, they just refuse to talk about them, especially in a family-enrichment setting.

Many programs targeting family life are based on pathology and counseling rather than on prevention and enrichment. Teaching persons skills to develop healthier relationships will enhance and enrich the lives of many who are not in need of therapeutic services.

Sadly, many couples endure a variety of tensions without reaching out for help or support from others. Most bypass opportunities offered in seminars, workshops, and presentations on child care or values orientation. An attitude of doing it alone deludes people into thinking they are doing it right, taking away any need to look at how well they are doing. Families are more likely to ask "Where did we go wrong?" than to ask how to avoid the common mistakes of marriage and family life.

With access to so many married couples, the church bears responsibility for what is happening in families today. There is nothing automatic about the quality of family life. What happens there, as anywhere, results from our specific efforts and at the cost of personal energy.

Courage to Love

"A lot of people get divorced who really don't want to," says Sandy. She and Mark were apart for two years.

"We still had feelings for each other," adds Mark, "and I knew we belonged together, but we had problems with our marriage. We felt we were the only ones with problems until we listened to others and realized they'd gotten themselves back together and were able to sit down and discuss and dialogue."

Couples in marital trouble often do not know where to turn. Trapped in the misery stage of a relationship, they feel no hope, blame each other for their pain, and fail to see each other because pain has made them turn in on themselves. Some fight a lot, while others hardly communicate.

Some spouses carry scars from an unhappy childhood that make relating in marriage difficult. They may never have had a stable relationship but thought, because they were in love, marriage would solve all the difficulties. Some carry unexpressed anger, others carry guilt, shame, fear, or insecurity, while still others have repressed their feelings. Some couples watched a fairly stable relationship deteriorate through busy-ness at work, alcoholism, infidelity, physical abuse, or drifting apart.

When couples reach out for help, they most often seek to solve a specific problem rather than to rebuild or strengthen their whole relationship. Professional counselors generally are forced by circumstances to focus on problems. That approach tends to be abstract and impersonal. Couples who simply try to solve problems will likely get hung up on the issues that have previously frustrated them. They need help to focus on persons and on feelings instead. Once a couple has a good relationship, they can usually solve their own problems or reach out together to someone who can help them. Counselors are much more effective when the couple's relationship is such they can approach the issues with a learning attitude rather than a defensive one.

Where does a couple turn when they face marital difficulties? Awareness that a problem exists is the first step toward change. But particular stresses and problems still stand in the way of intimacy. Powerful negative feelings have built over years. Resentments toward a spouse's actions, hurtful behaviors, and emotional unavailability have accumulated. Couples who have been together for a long time have deeply entrenched patterns of relating to one another.

Actually, couples in hurting relationships find it hard to get support to continue their marriage. Our society has created a climate for divorce. The common assumption is that people who suffer over an extended period of time in an unhappy marriage would do better to get out. Family and friends who see a couple in misery are more likely to encourage them to split than to work through the pain. Counselors, too, may seek to liberate them by encouraging them to end the marriage, failing to acknowledge the trauma of divorce. The persons best qualified to help are frequently peer ministers who share their own experience of pain and recovery. Every parish has a valuable resource in couples who went through extreme marital difficulty and are now in recovery. They are unlikely to come forward on their own, of course, failing to see the gift they have to share.

Family ministry is based on certain assumptions. One is that all families, no matter how fragmented and hurting, have tremendous strengths and the power to help and support other families. Another is that individuals and families who have been through a certain experience have a quality of caring and support to offer others in a similar situation that is unique and healing. The real experts in marriage and family ministry are spouses and family members. Sometimes specialized, professional help is needed, but the basic ministry lies in the day to day support that family members and peers give to each other. Such ministry flows from the mission of the family-centered church.

People expect the parish church to be there when they are hurting. Couples with marital trouble often have not experienced such care and help from priests so they do not turn to the pastoral staff. Any minister who discovers his or her ability to help family members face their real condition without fear or to make the decision to love in the face of painful human experience will be at the very center of people's lives.

Spirituality lies at the heart of healing and wholeness, especially a spirituality based on relationships rather than on the individual. Spirituality helps us get in touch with the God who cares, especially as that God is revealed in those persons closest to us. While a counselor believes in change in the individual and in the couple relationship, the minister believes in the working of God's grace in human lives and has faith that God can bring about transformations in people and in their relationships.

Care for hurting couples is a ministry of reconciliation, which places it at the center of church ministry. Yet the institutional church offers minimal help at this time. A few programs, most notably Retrouvaille, are now available, along with family counselors in a few parishes and a few qualified counselors among the clergy. Tragically, we devote more resources and energy to victims of divorce through support groups and efforts to annul broken marriages.

Divorce and Annulment

Not long ago, any woman asked, "Have you ever thought of divorcing him?," might answer, "Murder yes, divorce no!" Our high divorce rate now is fueled by our change in values and by failure to look at the reality of divorce. We too often act as if every infirm marriage ought to die, exchanging the traditional value of marriage for keeps with marriage until the passion fades. The more people accept the escape hatch, especially by putting conditions on their marriage at the start, the more people leave and the easier it becomes for others to follow. In an instamatic society, where we look at the short-term benefits of our actions, we can leave and feel better right away.

To view divorce as morally neutral, no better or worse than staying married, is damaging to those in difficulty. The trauma of divorce is oftimes worse than the marital disharmony. The lingering financial, emotional, and psychological effects are becoming apparent. Troubled couples easily become victims of propaganda from the media or from persons who work with hurting and broken marriages. After their divorce, they shape new relationships with the same lack of or distorted skills, and soon discover divorce was the wrong way to improve their lives.

Ministry to the separated and divorced has progressed more than any other family ministry in recent years. More parishes now sponsor support groups for the separated and divorced than for married couples or parents. Not long ago, divorced persons were like lepers in the Catholic community, and many left for other churches, so a more compassionate response is encouraging. However, we are literally pulling drowning bodies out of the stream rather than going upstream to stop people from falling in in the first place.

The process of divorce starts when a couple stops communicating verbally, sexually, and emotionally. Lack of or poor communication aggravates problems already present and unattended. Partners begin to find alternative sources of enjoyment, relaxation and support. When they give signs that the marriage is in difficulty and get no response, spouses may seek new confidants and friends to fill their relationship needs. Often one or the other will confront the relationship, which may lead to some efforts to get help, but by this time most people are encouraging the couple to separate.

Divorces happen in the misery stage of a relationship, when one or both spouses feel hurt and despair, lacking any hope for a better future. A person in the misery stage becomes quite self-protective, seeing the spouse as the source of his or her pain, which explains the blaming which goes on at this time. Lacking hope, this person easily decides to get out of the marriage. Many marriages could be reconciled at this time if the church were truly committed to marriage and family life.

The breakup of a marriage is also tragic for a couple's family and friends. When a part of their family system gets into trouble, children and extended family suffer. Their images and ideals are tarnished. People they counted on are letting them down. Divorce affects children's development, and causes symptoms of physical distress for both adults and children.

Sometimes people don't think children know what is going on, but they do. Children are listening hard to the fights in the bedroom and picking up the mood of their parents. In a dysfunctional family, where feelings aren't discussed, children may bottle up these insights for years and draw their own conclusions without ever discussing them with their parents. Meanwhile, the family message says everything is fine, forcing children to live the family secret. One parent may use children as confidants, seeking support against a spouse's transgressions.

Adults admit that during the intensely painful divorce process they were so absorbed by their own grief and the multitude of decisions to be made that they were not aware of how their children were reacting. Children perceive their parents' distress and may deliberately hide their own grief to avoid distressing the parent further. As far as children are concerned, "no-fault divorce" does not exist. They blame one parent or the other and they blame themselves for not being able to keep the marriage together.

For a long time we thought divorce did not have a serious impact on children and focused more on the expansion of freedom for adults. Studies on children of divorce indicate such harmful effects as school problems, psychological difficulties, drug abuse, suicide, out of wedlock pregnancies, and a tendency to also divorce last longer than once thought. The lasting effects, even on adult children, remind us that family ministry must be concerned about the entire family in a divorce.

The old argument of staying together for the sake of the kids has merit in many instances. We have not yet found an adequate substitute for the two parent family. Children need to learn the important lesson of facing problems rather than avoiding them. We may hesitate to develop preventive programs for fear of intruding on the automony of families, from an attitude that the problems families face are due to their own incompetence, or because of unwillingness to impose one set of values or model of family life on a variety of families. Yet the high emotional and financial cost of family breakdown suggests we must invest in saving marriages.

Divorced persons need a healing process beyond the civil divorce. The church's annulment process certainly opens old wounds, on which legal divorce might have put a temporary band-aid, but it can truly be part of an authentic healing. The annulment process asks a person to reflect on a broken relationship from its beginning to the bitter end, with an eye to forgiveness, reconciliation, and integration. It can do so only with the aid of a caring and supportive community.

Annulment is a costly process, which raises questions about how much time and money we should invest at this juncture in life as compared with preventive programs in the early years of marriage. However, granting an annulment also acknowledges our failure as a church toward marriage.

The annulment process helps heal the individual, family, and parish, as well as opening a new future for divorced persons. Through annulment ministry, the church extends to both parties the healing and reconciling presence of Jesus as well as the invitation to continue as active members in the church community. Unfortunately, the language of the church in the annulment process frequently causes difficulty, sounding more like a legal process than a sacramental or pastoral response.

Family ministers can help divorced Catholics realize that the annulment process is not a favor but a right to which they are entitled because of their membership in the church. The annulment process and the internal forum when a public declaration of nullity is not possible reflect the church's pastoral concern for its members. They witness the love and compassion of Christ revealed in the community of the church.

Remarriage in the Church

Before the end of this century more persons will be living in second and subsequent marriages than in first marriages. Persons seeking remarriage after divorce commonly feel fear, anger, defensiveness, and guilt which hint they are losers in a winner's society. While upholding permanence and commitment, the church should do everything possible to help persons choosing to remarry to enter into a healthy relationship. These persons need special preparation because of their brokenness and because they face such special issues as creating a new family with children.

A great deal of distorted thinking surrounds remarriage. One such myth is that divorce or death of a spouse ends the previous relationship. They do not. Death and divorce are often painful subjects easily ignored in the new relationship. Some expect love to be better the second time around; yet statistics are worse for second marriages than for first. Another illusion sees remarriage as between the spouses. A couple enters a complex network of in-laws, former spouses, children and other persons they must deal with. It takes a long time to develop new relationships within a family and the roles of stepmother and stepfather are not easily defined.

Many who plan remarriage find discussion of sensitive issues or potential problems very threatening. Mourning the loss of the previous relationship and separating emotionally from the previous spouse is a primary issue. So is changing family structures, from the single-parent family system to new roles in a new system. For the stepchild, remarriage of a parent frequently means the loss of a close parent-child relationship. Since the relationship of spouses is the most important factor in the new family, couples need time alone even though such time is more difficult to find than in first marriages.

The church has much to offer couples getting remarried. Our tradition of reconciliation and healing seems essential after the hurts and brokenness of failed relationships. This healing can be reflected in the wedding liturgy, e.g witnessing the bonding between members of the newly constituted family.

Remarried couples need a support community open to the likelihood that second marriages actually fulfill God's plan. Ministry to couples in second marriages also reflects our belief and concern for the permanence and sacramentality of marriage.

The church is about building relationships, especially in that primary community to which most people belong, the family. Individual family members live in the context of a series of relationships. A family perspective would sensitize us to the complexities of family life today, not as observers but as active participants in shaping the future of the family.

Actions to Consider

• Our pastoral concern is to foster lasting unions under God and to establish successful spiritual families. A good place to start is by developing a parish policy committed to marriage and family life. Such a policy might affirm the parish commitment to all families, while affirming belief in the permanence and sacramentality of marriage, goals for marriage preparation and enrichment, and strategies to help troubled marriages.

• Involve families with a major role in marriage preparation. Parents, grandparents and friends can be a part of this preparation by sharing their understanding of the sacrament, reflecting the seriousness of the upcoming marriage, and persuading the engaged to participate in the best marriage preparation possible. Marriage preparation belongs not only to the family but to the parish community where the couple are called to be a sacrament. Parishes could do more through sponsor couples before and after the wedding, good use of premarital inventories, and teaching biblical values on marriage.

• Parishes might join regionally in marriage preparation programs of quality. Parishes can become partners by finding couples to present these programs or by housing programs in their parish facilities. Parishes don't need to reinvent the wheel when good programs like Catholic Engaged Encounter and natural family planning programs are available. They play a major role in their success, however.

• Ministry to young marrieds is a great need in most parishes. Programs using sponsor couples on a one-to-one basis with quarterly meetings have worked. In Mexico City, Catholic Engaged Encounter successfully invites young marrieds to join support groups with their peers. Australia provides retreats for young marrieds. Most couples in their early years of marriage realize their need for and are open to support. More than programs, however, such ministry must emerge from a community that truly cares about its sacramental couples.

• Marriage enrichment and parenting programs are possible. What is needed in a parish is a plan to enrich and support marriages. Peer ministry using couples who share their stories and insights into marriage works. So does a parish mission focused on the family or days of enrichment. You might encourage couples to attend a married couples' retreat or Marriage Encounter outside the parish. You might invite the Christian Family Movement or Teams of Our Lady to set up support groups in the parish. The parish can be a resource creating awareness of programs already in the area. What we now lack is a plan and enthusiasm to carry it out.

• Parishes can also help couples in trouble. One priest asked to meet with couples whose marriages had been in serious trouble and were now in recovery. From this came a peer ministry program where these couples pair up with hurting couples looking for help. Some parishes have trained peer ministers for counseling. Others have hired a part or full time counselor who works with couples in need. Recovery programs, like Recovering Couples Anonymous and Troubled Couples Anonymous, might also be organized. All these multiply the availability of the church to help couples in trouble.

• A parish community can play a significant role in the annulment process. A program or retreat for those recently divorced might begin the healing and reconciling process within the church. Persons in marriages not blessed by the church might find an evening seminar on annulments helpful. A parish advocacy program with trained laypersons could support couples through the often intimidating annulment process. Persons going through the hurt and pain of divorce can benefit from a personal invitation to enter into the healing process, which gives a message that the church community cares about their personal and spiritual life. An ongoing divorced and separated group offers communal support, encouragement, and guidance to those who are just beginning their grieving or working through the annulment process.

4

The Family's Many Faces

As the National Conference of Catholic Bishops, we pledge to include more deliberately within the scope of our pastoral care an attentiveness to single-parent families, families in second marriages, grandparents raising children, interracial families, interfaith families and persons who are widowed or divorced.

THE AMERICAN DREAM AFTER WORLD WAR II ENVISIONED A family where mother stayed home to care for the children while Dad was the "good provider." Peter Marshall, a Presbyterian pastor in Washington, D.C., reminded Americans that "women come nearer to fulfilling their God-given function in the home than anywhere else." Marshall contended: "The breakdown of home life and influence will mark the breakdown of the nation."

The nuclear family became the socially-approved model because its structure fit well the needs of a mass-production society with widely shared values and lifestyles, hierarchical power, and a clear separation of home life from work. Recently drastic social forces have changed the face of the American family. Economic conditions, feminism, and a career mentality are among reasons many women have left the home for the workplace. Values also changed, e.g., from a focus on child well-being to adult well-being and happiness, with less than half the adults now regarding sacrifice for others as a positive virtue. The media increasingly depicts the married two-parent family as a pathological source of abuse, incest, and violence. Many studies, however, clearly link the nuclear family unit with the well-being of the nation.

Obviously, most households do not fit the American ideal today. The *New York Times* reported in 1989 that "New York's highest court, the Court of Appeals, ruled in July that a gay couple who had lived together for a decade could be considered a family under New York City's rent-control regulations. The Court said the protection for eviction, previously granted only to people related by blood, marriage or adoption, 'should not rest on fictitious legal distinctions or genetic history, but instead should find its foundation in the reality of family life.'"

Some large cities now have domestic partnership laws, which require benefits like family health insurance and paid bereavement leave be paid to employees who live as unmarried couples. Such changes make it more difficult to define the family. Dr. Pat Voydanoff of Dayton University writes: "In the past, a family was seen as an economic unit, important for economic exchanges such as inheritance. More recently, families have been perceived as a psychological unit."*

It gets very difficult to discuss changes in family structure without provoking angry responses, such as accusations of attacking single parent families or harboring racial and religious prejudice. I will not attempt to determine the definition of family, but to note that the traditional church paradigm of the "good Catholic family" as an intact family of Dad, Mom and multiple kids certainly creates a barrier to family ministry in today's parish. Our generation is not witnessing the end of the nuclear family, as the prophets of doom warn us; yet the nuclear family no longer defines the standard for society. Raised to believe the nuclear family was both the ideal and normal family, while others' were somehow suspect if not deviant, many Americans remain intolerant to the new variety in family styles. Our laws, welfare practices, school arrangements and housing codes all remain implicitly biased toward the nuclear family. They take little account of or subtly discriminate against women who work, of men who stay home to care for their children, of single-parent families, and of single persons.

---

* Sarah Miller, Ed., "The Family," *Overview*, Vol. 25, No. 24 (April, 1991), p. 2.

Family structure is an explosive issue for most of us. We debate over deeply held and conflicting values. We believe in equality and diversity against evidence that suggests that not all family structures produce equal outcomes for children. We value the freedom of adults to pursue individual happiness in their private relationships, even though we feel the needs of children for stability, security and permanence in their family lives. These difficult issues generate conflict in the debate over family life today.

Three assumptions supported our acceptance of the changing family. Economically, Americans developed a belief that women could make it on their own, that equality for women lay in the world of work outside the home, and that working women were more fulfilled than women who stayed at home. We also assumed that family disruption would not cause lasting harm to children and could even enrich their lives. Identifying progress with a growing tolerance for diversity, Americans saw the expansion of individual opportunities for choice, freedom, and self-expression as making this a better society.

How does the church fit into this picture? Families need help to adjust to the rapid changes. Sydney Callahan reminds us that a domesticated church inevitably tends to become conservative, class conscious, sexist, and ineffectual in the society at large. Does this mean the church cannot vitally serve this wide diversity of family types? The mission of the church must be to transcend and support the family, believing that all families can enrich the life of the church. *Such mission awareness demands that we shift our paradigm from the rigid "good catholic family" model to one which, while affirming the special value of the intact nuclear family, embraces the reality and strengths of diverse family types that comprise the church.* In reality, the church's mindset on family life is far less significant than its lack of involvement with families.

The stabilizing influence of churches and other institutions on marriage and family life has diminished. Opposing views of marriage as a call from God focused on the welfare of society or as a private agreement between two individuals for their enjoyment and satisfaction create tension. Increasingly, couples view marriage as a two-party contract that can be terminated when either party desires.

Families have had to adapt and change throughout history. Fortunately, the family is adaptable, able to change its roles and structures to thrive in the midst of bewildering and negative forces. Today's families experience intense growing pains as they stretch to keep up with rapid changes, including the influence of the mass media, a mobile lifestyle, an influx of races other than Europeans, the need for women to go outside the home to work, the greying of America, divorce, single-parenthood, and blended families. While family breakdown has indeed been accompanied by serious social decay, there are success stories such as single parents rearing children with strong values. The church needs to affirm families, building their confidence rather than adding guilt and fear.

We have been taught that most of the problems experienced by families have their origin within the family and therefore ought to be solved by the individual family member primarily concerned. We have looked less clearly at how our social institutions determine the conditions of life for our families and their children. Church, school and workplace need to look at their role in support of families rather than take the one-sided view that families exist as a unit of support for church, school and workplace. This chapter looks not so much at sociological realities as at the church's response. The church must go through changing pains right along with the family.

Multi-Cultural, Multi-Racial Families

Not many years ago, the marriage of a black American to a white American shocked the whole community. Now the startling fact is the extent to which persons from widely different cultural and racial backgrounds marry each other. We have come to accept this as an expression of the American belief in tolerance and social opportunity. A church that affirms marriage as a vocational call from God has to allow that God would call persons of varying ethnic and cultural backgrounds to enjoy each other. Yet that church must also be concerned about the consequences of such marriages.

Interracial and intercultural marriages often create unique difficulties for the couple, their family, and their friends. Relatives, who play a vital role in making and breaking marriages, may find their standards and beliefs so threatened that they reject their son or daughter. The couple often face unexpected discrimination in housing, employment, and job advancement. Finding themselves distanced from their families, they may live in isolation, unable to join in the social and cultural life of their families. Couples may hesitate to have children because they fear social ostracism will hurt their child.

Couples entering an interracial or intercultural marriage deserve support from the church community and pastoral staffs. Before marriage, the all-important exploration of motives requires a special sensitivity on the part of family, friends, and clergy. These couples frequently feel loneliness and guilt when their marriage is frowned on by both family and church.

Couples in intercultural and interracial marriages are generally aware of society's unfavorable attitude. Family and church members help by being respectful of the culture differing from their own or harm by prejudices and negative attitudes. Feeling uncomfortable in many congregations, these couples easily become disillusioned and turn away from their church.

Interdenominational Marriages

In the 1960s, Catholic Youth Organization leaders urged Catholics to date only Catholics while Luther League leaders urged Lutherans to date only Lutherans. While some parents still urge their children to date within their denomination, most are more concerned about raising children who are drug-free and motivated for life. Churches say too little about potential difficulties.

Interdenominational marriages may be between two Christians or a Christian with someone from another religious background. Estimates say up to 60% of Catholics marry someone of another religious tradition, with or without the church's approval. Once viewing such persons almost as traitors, Catholics now recognize that the fault lies not with the couple but with the split among Christians. Most couples tend to minimize the effects of religious differences, perhaps finding them too confusing, threatening, or painful to face.

What happens to these marriages today? A few remain successfully rooted in two different faith communities. A fair number join a common denomination. The larger number end up becoming indifferent or with only one participating in a faith community. The divorce rate among interdenominational marriages is high, but divorce seems more connected with religious indifference than with religious difference.

For churches, the most frequent question is "How can we be of help to the family where only one spouse participates in the life of the church?" Not long ago, churches urged the conversion of one partner as a solution. Interdenominational couples faced divisive problems with baptism and religious education of their children. Pastoral responses often left couples feeling their marriages were an aberration rather than a gift to the churches.

How should we view interdenominational marriages? Certainly not as second-rate marriages, when two people are responding to God's call. The question revolves around to what God calls them in their faith journey. Is God speaking to the churches about the split in the Body of Christ? Do couples where each spouse participates actively in his or her church and shares in the religious education of their children offer an example of a new paradigm for restoration of Christian unity? Is it possible that Christian partners in interdenominational marriages are making a quiet but profound ecumenical statement about their identity as members of the one church with distinct traditions, even as they experience the scandal of the divided churches? Could these families have navigated a paradigm shift that makes possible an experience of the future church?

If God calls a couple to unity in their marriage, could we also conclude that faith certainly forms a most important element of that unity? God would not want the human split in the Body of Christ to destroy a couple's marriage. Spiritual unity may be possible for spouses from different denominations when both have openness, understanding, and recognize the strengths as well as the weaknesses of both denominations. Unfortunately, most couples do not seem able to cope well with such differences. A split that seemed insignificant at the time of the wedding looms larger when questions of intercommunion, participation in each other's faith community, and moral issues divide their lives. Couples have the difficult task of creating a united Christian home in a divided church which pulls them in two directions and may not welcome them effectively to each other's congregation. The churches help such couples remain spiritual singles.

Karin refused to enter into a religiously split marriage, remembering holidays as the most painful time in her childhood, when her Lutheran father and Catholic mother would fight over who would take the children to church. *Such stories readily argue for a paradigm where God calls couples to avoid being victims of the split among churches by embracing a common church membership.* Religious leaders point to the strength of such couples who made an adult decision to practice their faith in one denomination. Terri and Bo believe God may be calling spouses to at least heal the division in their family centered church: "We feel very strongly about the need for couples to go to church together. We never felt any spiritual unity in our marriage until we were able to share God and church with each other."

A growing privatism regarding religion in American culture shapes another concern. A 1988 Gallup survey revealed 80% of Americans agreed that "an individual should arrive at his or her own religious beliefs independent of any churches or synagogues." Such privatism erodes the connection between the family and the church community. It also creates difficulties between generations since, of all the pains of parenting, children's rejection of parental values seems the most painful.

Dual-Career Families

Debates over legislation affecting families often focus on the Ozzie and Harriet model of family life, leaving out a majority of American families. Nowhere is this more apparent than in the growing number of two-jobs-outside-the-home families. Changes in family life, such as fathers taking on added household and parenting responsibilities, need for outside child care, and latch-key children demand our attention.

More than half of all mothers with preschool children worked outside the home in 1991, compared with only one in five in 1960. For families, this means little time for outside activities, play, or spiritual renewal, as well as isolation from the extended family and friends, guilt over parenting, need to schedule time for romance and sexuality, and need for support systems. This causes stress, leaving women frequently feeling like victims pulled between two full time jobs in the career and at home while fathers mull over questions about unbounded career demands and parenting time in their children's most formative years. As Francine and Douglas Hall note: "Most fights over women's rights take place in the kitchen, not in the State Capitol."*

As couples try to clarify their roles and tasks within a a two-career marriage, churches cling rather tightly to 1950s ideal for the family. Yet women were traditionally part of the work force, only they generally worked alongside their husbands on the farm or in the shop rather than away from home. Women tended to stay behind when industrialization took men away from home.

The women's movement has raised some very basic questions about jobs and self-worth. We undervalue the economic contribution of family responsibilities, pay women only about two-thirds as much as men, and expect them to take service jobs. Women are thought to have less commitment to their job due to the demands of raising a family and the likelihood of a move with their husbands. Care for sick children, school in-service days, and trips to the dentist are thought to diminish the employee's full value to the company. Sexual hassassment on the job, the availability of child care, maternity leaves, and the limited protection afforded to part-time workers affect women's employment.

Despite role ambiguity and the pressures women face in juggling careers, job and family, the workplace offers continu-

---

* Hall, Francine and Hall, Douglas T., *The Two-Career Family* (Reading, MA: Addison-Wesley Publishing Co., 1979), p. 113.

ing appeal even beyond the income. Work has come to supply our worth. Wages convey society's worth and self-identity for the individual. Women work for social contacts, for future security, and for personal growth and development as well.

The women's issue clearly impacts on family ministry. Ministers can no longer identify women's vocation almost exclusively with motherhood and care of the home, even though some argue this is women's role. The desire to own a house and other economic needs make one-wage-earner families frequently impossible. Putting work first may sometimes stem from a selfish desire to prove oneself in the world of work or to have unnecessary material goods, but simple answers aren't enough. We need a healthy dialogue within the church about the questions and problems facing women in the world of work as well as homemaking.

Men as well as women are burdened by conflicting demands. Caring for children and finding time for each other becomes an impossible equation. Fortunately, many men remember their fathers as too busy to have much time for them and deliberately spend more time in child-care as well as household tasks. They need a more family friendly work environment, with family emergency leave, job sharing, and flexible work schedules. Will the church, which once worked with unions to bring about eight hour workdays, the abolition of child labor, and just wages, now lead the fight for pro-family reforms?

Mobile Families

In pre-industrial times, work was a major means of personal identity. People spent most of their waking hours from childhood to death in the craft shop or on the farm, taking great pride that their work was God-given. American families must now be more mobile, frequently needing to be retrained for new tasks several times during their lifetime.

With their extended family now spread over several states, people rely more on the nuclear family and other communities for relationships. Friendships often are disturbed when a family uproots itself for a job transfer or to pursue a better job. More and more, we become a nation of strangers.

Families typically take several years to become part of a new faith community after a move. Can the church develop a more sensitive way to find potential new members who move into the area, to effectively welcome new arrivals, and to keep contact by a previous parish until families plug into a new parish family?

Some dioceses and parishes already have programs for migrant laborers and experience with ministry to military families which can provide helpful insights for ministering to mobile families. Most parishes have commuter families, with a worker away from home for days or weeks at a time. Affirming these difficult issues of space and time can help these families to feel welcome without making them feel guilty for not being more involved.

Single-Parent Families

Nearly one in eight families was headed by a single parent in 1991, with that parent five times more likely to be a woman. About a quarter of all children, nearly three times that of 1960 or more than 16 million of them, lived with only one parent in 1991. Well over half of all children will spend part of their growing up years with a single parent. This growing number of single-parent families reflects a rise in divorce and unmarried parenthood. Single parents face special ongoing tasks such as fulfilling the role of both parents, child custody questions, living on a decreased income, moves for cheaper housing and better jobs, time management, difficulty sustaining ties to family and friends, and finding adequate child care.

Contrary to the common stereotype that depicts children of single-parent households as troubled and socially maladjusted, many single parents do an excellent job of raising their children. Parenting becomes more difficult, so solo parents need more creativity, more consistency, a strong sense of self-esteem, and support from the community. The breakup of parents gets especially difficult for teenagers when it comes to trusting friends of the opposite sex enough to develop a love relationship. Lack of self-confidence seems to be the most profound and widespread effect of divorce upon children, permeating the daily life of single parents as well. Churches generally do not provide good support for single parents. Most parishes reflect the institutional church's unaccepting attitude toward either divorce or pregnancy outside of marriage. Single parents, expecting the church's moral judgment rather than the compassion of Jesus, are not likely to approach the church for support.

The single-parent family certainly falls among those needy persons for whom the bible asks us to be an advocate. Parents and children need to feel valued and cared for, to experience a loving and faithful God who sustains each of us even in time of overwhelming needs. They would prefer to be accepted for who they are and what they can offer the parish rather than seen as deficient families. Single-parent families need to feel the church recognizes their needs and values their presence, especially after facing people's judgment and insensitivity. Fortunately, the Beginning Experience Weekend and parish-based support groups for the separated, divorced, and widowed represent significant progress in the church's response to these families in recent years.

Blended Families

In 1991, one in three people was a member of a stepfamily. That number is expected to rise to nearly one in two by the turn of the century. Research indicates that children living with stepparents are even less stable than those in single-parent homes. Stepfamilies disrupt loyalties, create new uncertainties, and sometimes threaten the child's physical safety as well as emotional security.

It is easy to believe that when we love someone, we will love their children, and marriage will put our family back together the way it should be. For a child, the marriage of a parent often provokes confused feelings of sadness, anger and rejection. The complicated dynamics of blended family units with children deserve sensitive pastoral care and support.

Catholics are divorcing today at near the normal rate for all Americans and many will remarry. Persons often drop out of sight or find another congregation where they are unknown when marital breakup occurs. Many remarried families are entirely churchless. They may not believe the church has a place for them or anything to offer them. We as a church need to ask forgiveness for our shortcomings that often made it difficult for spouses to live a sacramental marriage.

Religion is often the biggest problem for remarried Christians. They view the church as anti-divorce and anti-remarriage, frequently feeling a need to choose between their church and remarriage. Many have a sense of their initial vows as permanent and feel hypocritical asking for an annulment. Failure in marriage often creates feelings that God would want nothing more to do with the person. Consequently, many marry civilly without seeking the church's help, torn with questions about membership and Eucharist.

Remarriage means new family structures. After a death or divorce, a new single-parent family system develops. Remarriage brings major role changes, perhaps with expectations family members will embrace roles from previous family relationships. Stepmothers who try to be "supermoms" may find themselves resisted or resented by children who have grown used to more self-sufficiency. Stepfathers are often blind to the complexity of the situation and try to take control immediately. The unspoken assumption is that the stepfather's role is no role at all.

Ex-spouses tend to compete for the loyalty of their children. Stepfamily members need to develop new boundaries in areas such as bringing friends into the home, discussing family problems, and handling step-sibling conflicts. Blended families need a good support system, another parish opportunity.

Childless Marriages

In 1991, the most common family unit was the married couple with no children at home. 42% of all families, they included couples in various situations – younger couples planning to have children, older couples whose children have left home, couples involuntarily childless or intentionally child-free. Their number is growing rapidly.

Few couples without children are found in the church, even among those who had a devout upbringing. Quite likely they do not sense a hospitable environment in a strongly pro-child church. This challenges the church to work on its theology of child-freeness, seeing sexual love in marriage as good in and of itself. Biblical teachings appear to favor the side of childbearing. Barrenness brought women sorrow and disdain, while children helped a woman to achieve her true purpose in life, an insight questioned by married couples today.

Each child created in the image of God deserves to be born into a home that has time, interest, and resources to provide for it. Persons can be creative without being procreative, finding value and meaning in life in ways other than childbearing. Some couples may not be called to be parents because of their genes, gifts, or graces. Willingness to give of self to persons other than children, e.g., to social causes, seems sufficient for a valid marital union. Couples grieving the child they will never have need rituals and church services as surely as couples who experience the joy of new life. Right now much of the church's energy and time is focused on the needs of children. Childless couples deserve to know if they are also important.

Multi-Generational Families

The four generation family is now the norm in America. Ironically, these generations often do not live anywhere near each other. Consequently, the elderly feel isolated and alone, adults are overburdened with caring for both children and the older generation, and children barely know their grandparents and great-grandparents because they rarely see them.

Several factors contribute to the present isolation of family members. Mobility means most adult children no longer live in the neighborhood of their parents. An extended lifespan means that many elderly couples and singles find themselves alone, often reluctant to be a "burden" on their children because they earlier experienced their parents saddled with an elderly relative without any supportive services. It also means that we have many retired couples with time for leisure and volunteerism.

In a previously agrarian society, older persons frequently cared for young children while the younger adults engaged in productive work. Grandparents in the Native American tradition are the teachers of children, giving the elderly a vital role in the family. Grandparents and grandchildren often feel close bonds differing from those between parent and child.

Opportunities for grandparents to feel useful or to establish bonds with their grandchildren are less common today. Some expressly do not want to be tied down or taken advantage of as babysitters by their grown children, but many would love to care in this way if only they lived close enough.

"The continuity of all cultures," says Margaret Mead, "depends on the living presence of at least three generations." We learn how to be parents, e.g., in a particular cultural context. If one generation is missing, cultural values and practices are not likely to be expressed or continued. The presence of older generations is deeply reassuring, especially in troubled and rapidly changing times. Older people gain a sense of having lived a meaningful life when they see younger generations profiting from what they have accomplished. Close contact helps the older generations to feel that younger generations are not so different from themselves.

Suburban housing often groups families of a similar age. Students and young workers may go for weeks without contact with the elderly. Retired persons frequently choose senior housing, appearing there to be more active, have higher morale and greater neighborhood mobility. The elderly are more likely to fear contacts with teenagers than to welcome them. Children learn not to trust the friendly overtures of adult strangers. Most parents prefer not to live with their adult children, but will accept it if forced by circumstances. The rapid change in our society can sharpen differences between age groups, contributing to a sense of uniqueness among members of each age group.

Early retirement and patterns of hiring have narrowed the age range at the workplace so much that some companies are establishing mentoring programs to build contact between experienced and younger employees. Recreational and social-service programs use age as a criterion for determining eligibility for participation. Few institutions offer the opportunity for a broad range of participation. The church is one of the major ones which still welcomes persons of all ages.

Churches that think intergenerationally can increase contact between the various age groups. The family-centered church is a prime place for this ministry. Children who live with or share frequent contact with frail, elderly relatives come to understand their limitations and to make themselves useful. Being the primary caregiver for elderly or infirm parents can place a strain on the family. Because families provide the bulk of medical and personal care for the elderly, most children will face difficult decisions at some time. Do they continue a career or stay at home and provide care? How do they maintain healthy relationships with other family members? Persons more often care for their parents at a distance rather than have these experiences in their own homes nowadays. Ministers need to be sensitive for the complex questions and stresses surrounding intergenerational issues.

Singles

The experiences of being single in the church are varied. Many factors determine how persons react to being single, such as their relationship with God, how they become single, their level of self-esteem, and whether they experience society and the church accepting of singles. Many singles feel everything in the church is geared toward the family. Emphasis on family gives them a sense they are viewed as abnormal.

It is critical that family ministers address the single households of the parish as well. Sometimes it seems from a family minister's perspective that little is happening for families in a parish, but from a single person's perspective family-related topics are all he or she ever hears about. Single persons, of course, generally have a network of family relationships that continue to be important.

The typical parish fails to adequately address relationship issues unique to the single person's vocation. Needs vary too. Young singles have different needs than those called to remain single for life, who bear the stigma of being labelled "never married." The divorced single adult is least understood. Older, perhaps widowed, single people generally elicit automatic support and sympathy from the church.

By placing young people into youth groups, parishes may make life easier for adults but adulthood harder for youth. The youth group then becomes part of the problem rather than part of the solution. Setting youth apart in this way sets up the very kind of market conditions that the media need to reach youth. Youth mature better by working with adults, accomplishing something that will build their self-esteem. We best get youth into the mainstream of the parish not just as representatives but as members who are becoming adults and have something to offer.

Listening, as usual, is most important for parish staffs. Persons attempting to launch a singles ministry program may assume they know what single persons want and need. This results in a social club approach few single people find attractive. Parish congregations need to hear more about single life as a unique and important vocation in the church. Christian single life can be very meaningful. Pursuit of a celibate calling in everyday life enables one to be more abidingly present to all who need care. When singles find themselves alone, laughed at, isolated, or at odds with a society and church that does not welcome their efforts to witness to the value of single life in Christ, they may feel overwhelmed by a desire to escape it all.

Single parenting is taking a new unexpected twist among churchgoing singles. Single women are deciding to adopt children. Other single women are fed up with unstable relationships and bypass adoption to give birth to their own child. In some parishes, e.g., the African-American community, singles ministry takes on added significance due to the tragic reality that so many black males leave women without partners.

One other group deserving the church's ministry, no matter what our judgment of their lifestyle, is the growing number of committed homosexual relationships. Likely, such loyal, permanent relationships will increase as AIDS fears change sexual practice away from the casual toward the committed. If the population of gays and lesbians is about 10% of the population as a whole, many families are touched because they love these family members even as the institutional church seems to reject or neglect them.

In specific, Christianity has taken for granted that sexual intercourse signifies a commitment to offspring and, therefore, the naturalness of male-female intercourse. Since we no longer link intercourse so explicitly with offspring, however, what has been taken for granted can no longer function as a guideline. Certainly, the church has difficulty regarding homosexual unions as a cause for public celebration and rejoicing. Likely the church's thinking on this will not change soon, even when mutual consent between the partners may be present.

All in the Family

In perplexing times, family ministers might well wish for the wisdom of Jesus. Obviously, Jesus reached out to a diversity of people with compassion and love. Can the church be any less compassionate to families under pressure? When we read about families in previous generations, we realize that the same dread warnings about the demise of the family appear. Yet the family doesn't die. It changes to combat the pressures and strains of its moment in history.

Traditional values like trust, respect, support, kinship, responsibility, and faith are highly valued by the family units described in this chapter. The challenge these families face lies in retaining their values in the midst of a culture that seems bent on destroying them. Families are struggling hard to foster these values and many are succeeding, but they aren't getting the help they need from the institutions.

How are we to assess the family trends of recent decades? While recognizing that two-parent families may not always be possible and many are dysfunctional, and many non-traditional families are successful and deserve our support, we do well to consider the 1988 National Health Interview Survey of Child Health, which found that "young people from single-parent families or stepfamilies were two or three times more likely to have emotional or behavioral problems than those who had both of their biological parents present in the home."[*]

A symbiotic relationship between the family and the parish makes the health of one depend upon the health of the other. Family ministers need to help the diversity of families recognize how they can better impact on the parish. Parish staffs ready to meet their needs must first change from a rigid paradigm based on the nuclear family to one embracing the wide diversity of today's families. Parishes need to change from an educational child-centered basis to one where families learn that they have power to initiate change and share a responsibility for solutions. They also need to help families deal with the frustration of not being heard even when they offer solutions, so they do not give up but continue to seek ways to bring pressure to bear for healthy change. Many ministers need to resist an attitude which sees the family as an institutional nuisance so they view the family rather as an institutional resource which holds out hope for a loving church of the future. Otherwise, the church may actually contribute to family instability and breakup.

Actions to Consider

• Here is where parish ministers must seek first to understand, to listen to the needs of diverse families. Be aware of how our paradigms of family get in the way of understanding. Unless we listen with an clear intent to understand, we hear others and prescribe solutions though our own experiences.

• Parishes generally could do better ministry to interdenominational couples in marriage preparation and during the marriage. Failure often causes a lot of pain, anger and frustration for couples struggling with this division. Invite interdenominational couples to be involved in marriage preparation. Jointly sponsor with other churches a retreat for interdenominational couples. Invite the partner of another faith to come forward at communion time to receive a blessing. Pray for the unity of Christians so that you are a reminder of the painful split in the Body of Christ. Urge these couples to seek a strong unity in their faith life as a family centered church.

** Quoted by David Popenoe, "Don't Believe the Criticism About Two-Parent Families, *Minneapolis Star*, (December 31, 1992), p. 19.

• The church faces lots of possibilities to help dual-career families. It might conduct a retreat weekend or support group for the two-career couple, exploring skills to renegotiate appropriate roles in marriage. The church might link couples with similar needs: e.g., parishes might offer support groups to help jobless people through the discouraging task of job hunting. A day-care program or an after-school program with competent, compassionate care for children would be welcomed. The parish might also examine its employment policies to see how they show sensitivity and flexibility for two-career couples.

• Church leaders do well to communicate an understanding that the single-parent family can be a strong, stable family unit. Marriage seems so esteemed in the church that single parents feel they are on the fringes. The parish can contribute by linking single-parent families with other caring families. Such concern helps them overcome the guilty feelings of being second-class for having failed to reach the ideals the church espouses. Parish staff best be sensitive to the harsh economic conditions of most single-parent families, realizing how church programs may create an economic hardship. These families need to be invited to participate in church life, peer groups, and volunteerism, although for short-term projects because of time limitations.

• Churches have done relatively little to meet the mutual needs of several age groups by planning activities across generational lines. Intergenerational programs between retired, older persons and the very young, and between older children and the frail elderly have proved successful in some parishes. Such links are badly needed where we live in such an increasingly age-segregated society that we lack a sense of community. Parishes might sponsor support groups of older women who can form maternal mentoring relationships with younger mothers, help isolated or single-parent families to include a grandparent from the congregation in family holidays, or set up a program where elderly can get some needed chores done while teenagers can provide services and learn skills at the same time.

• The elderly are often lost to any parish congregation. Many gave up their homes to move into senior housing or a condo away from the area where they raised their family. Often in ill health or unable to get out, many do not join the local parish. Parishes need to find ways to identify the elderly who move into their area so they might provide ministry for them.

• Persons remarrying need special marriage preparation. Our tradition of reconciliation and healing is very necessary after the hurts and brokenness of failed relationships. This healing can be reflected in the wedding liturgy, as can bonding between members of the newly constituted family. Serious ministry to these couples can reflect the compassionate work of Jesus while making a strong statement that we really do believe in and strive for permanence.

5

Ordinary Holiness

The profound and ordinary moments of daily life –
mealtimes, workdays, vacations, expressions of love
and intimacy, household chores, caring for a sick
child or elderly parent, or even conflicts over things
like how to celebrate holidays, discipline children or
spend money – all are the threads from which you
can weave a pattern of holiness.

IN 1977, A GROUP OF CATHOLICS ISSUED THE CHICAGO DECLARATION
of Christian Concern, charging that emphasis on institutional
church-related activities was overshadowing the role of the laity in their daily lives. One signer, Ed Marciniak, said: "I did
not sign the Chicago Declaration because I felt that the laity has
been pushed around, stepped upon, crushed by some ecclesiastical yoke or an authoritarian pastor; my signature was there
because we laity have been ignored. Indifference has been our
lot. Our vocation was seen an unimportant. Our workaday
world has been slighted. Where in recent years have you
heard the vocation of the rank-and-file Christians celebrated?"[*]
    As we approach the twenty-first century, many Catholics
still feel they hear little in church on Sunday morning relevant
to their life during the week. The gap between Sunday and
Monday, between faith and daily life, still plagues us. The
meaning of life is either lost or found in one's daily routines.
Faith makes little sense apart from what goes on in the daily
experiences of family relationships, work, public life and leisure activities. Finding the sacred in the secular does not
mean that we abandon prayer and worship, but that we experience all of life as related to God's presence and activity.

---

[*]   Quoted in *Challenge to the Laity* (Huntington, Ind.: Our Sunday
Visitor, Inc, 1980), p. 35.

It is hard to see the holy in washing dirty laundry, wiping runny noses, fighting freeways, boring jobs, community tensions, advertising propaganda, and the complexities of modern family life. Dehumanizing work often alienates people. We clutter our leisure time with a consumer mentality and busy-ness that keep us from rest and relationships. Our theology and spirituality were centered outside of ordinary life. If people fail to hear their daily life has any significance, they are left with a schizophrenic view that separates faith from other areas of their lives.

A major paradigm shift whould change our view from a holy church saving members out of an unholy world to an awareness of the potential holiness in the ordinary. We then search for God in all of life, not simply in sacraments, worship and prayer. We find holiness as readily in life in the family centered church as in the Sunday church. This radical shift is complicated by the loss of so many symbols once considered sacred while yet unable to identify new symbols in what we previously thought secular.

Connecting Faith and Life

For years pastoral leaders have assumed that if there are adequate programs for gathering, the faithful will naturally find effective means for relating faith to daily life. Pastoral leaders focus on getting people involved in parish activities. But the church is a community of people who gather to be dispersed to bring Christ's presence to the factories, shops, homes, and city council chambers of the community.

Laity are in the world as church. Their daily experience in work, politics, family and community life is the setting for their Christian faith and spirituality. This experience of church must be drawn into the parish, affirmed, reflected upon, and celebrated. Decisions that determine the future of our children, the use of our finite resources, our relationship to other nations, and perhaps even the future of life on our planet are made in board rooms and government offices by Christians who are often embarrassed by their values and decisions.

Faith is not simply the knowledge of God that we learn as children or adults. Faith is a relationship that grows as we experience the movement of God at key moments in our lives, such as sitting in a foxhole, falling in love, having a baby, or standing at the bedside of a dying parent. Diedrich Bonhoeffer reminded us: ". . . it is only by living completely in the world that one learns to have faith. . . . By this worldliness I mean living unreservedly in life's duties, problems, successes and failures, experiences and perplexities. In so doing we throw ourselves completely into the arms of God."*

In faith, we aren't certain what we really know so we seek to get deeper into the reality around us. Yet, much of our time and energy are devoted to numbing ourselves to an openness and vulnerability to God. When the living God surges through reality and brings us to consciousness, it's a moment of hope and of possible change. God is asking us to be born through the frustrations, tears, joys, celebrations, laughter, feelings and experiences of daily life. The church, however, has been skeptical of personal experience.

To connect faith and life, we need a spirituality that is focused on this world and not otherworldly. Bishop Kenneth Untener reminds us that "The church has never attempted to relate to the world as we are today. . . . The shaping of this world is part of the process of shaping the kingdom. . . . The further the church reaches outward, the more it must be true to its center, who is Christ. And the more it is true to its center, the more it reaches outward."**

Faith sees grace present in the most elementary acts of life. It ritualizes them and raises them to the sacramental level. Daily life is full of sacraments, sacred signs signifying and effecting God's presence. A garden, a friendship, an act of reconciliation or a family heirloom can become sacraments for us. The world is ultimately a sacrament of God. Sacraments are deeply rooted in human life. In the reality of our lives, we discover another Reality.

---

* Diedrich Bonhoeffer, *The Cost of Discipleship* (New York: Macmillan, 1959), p. 169.
** Address to the Conference of Major Superiors of Men, *Origins*, (Sept. 11, 1986), pp. 240-241.

Experience of God is always a sacramental experience. Everything is or can become a sacrament. It depends on the way we look at things. Everything is a sacrament from God's viewpoint. A sacrament does not tear us away from our world, but asks us to look more closely and deeply into the very heart of the world. The world will then be transmuted into an eloquent sacrament of God. Sacramental thinking means that the roads we travel, the houses in our neighborhood, and the persons in our community are not simply people, houses and roads like all others in the world. They are part of ourselves, the sacraments in our lives.

In separating the sacred from the ordinary, we have lost the ancient Hebrew view that all creation is good, with humans created in the image of the Creator. The early church knew very well that outward rituals signified something deeply spiritual. Jesus was God made visible, the first sacrament. The church was the second great sacrament, thus being church is the starting point for all sacramental theology. St. Augustine, who defined sacrament as "a visible form of invisible grace," named hundreds of actions and things as sacraments. The hierarchical church came to see sacraments as the action of its priests, ultimately narrowing this to seven ritual actions in the twelfth century.

Grace is a relationship with God, not a quality; something we live creatively rather than receive passively. In the broad range of Christian activity that is sacrament, probably the most basic is human love, which is sacramental of divine love. Recognizing divine energy and grace in the simple and intimate things of everyday life is our first act of faith and the beginning of our sacramental understanding. Until pastoral staffs help people to understand the sacramentality of all life, they will scarcely understand the weak symbols of the church's seven sacraments of faith, which radicalize the natural sacraments we experience in our daily lives.

The Loss of the Sacred

Most Catholics know little of the history concerning separation of the sacred and the secular, and why most attention in the church has been given to the hierarchy, clergy and religious while the majority of members were neglected. For the early Christians, Jesus was alive and at work in the believing community in which he was now enfleshed. Peter reminded early believers: "You, however, are 'a chosen race, a royal priesthood, a holy nation, a people he claims for his own . . . ' Once you were no people, but now you are God's people" (1 Peter 2: 9-10).

Before long we see beginnings of an institutional church and the emergence of a distinct clerical group. This did not quickly diminish the role of ordinary people, who shared the good news through their life and work, but we begin to see an early identification of the mission of Jesus with the ministry of the hierarchy. Persecutions afflicted the church very early, backing the hierarchy away from trying to Christianize secular affairs, and leaving the cobblers, woolworkers and ordinary people to risk carrying the gospel into the recesses of society.

In the second century, when western Christians developed a strong interest in Greek thought, Gnosticism became a strange bedpartner. Gnostic dualism divided the world into two realms, namely matter which was evil and spirit which was good. It separated material creation from its Creator, and stressed higher and lower divisions such as the soul over the body, the church over the world, and contemplation over action. Over the years the church developed elaborate schemes for the ascent of the soul from the body. Ascetical practices and escape from sensuality replaced emphasis on love and community.

Gnosticism's effect on the church has been profound. Wendell Berry calls this division between the holy and the world, which separated the Creator from creation, "perhaps the greatest disaster in human history." This way of viewing life in terms of opposites led to the distinction of clergy versus laity, and even men versus women. A mentality of higher and lower rankings fostered competion and control rather than cooperation. Clergy and religious escaped from the world to spend their energies on divine things while the laity had to be involved in the secular and unholy world. Major effects followed the distinction of the spiritual from the material. Work, seen as co-creation with the Creator in the Old Testament, now became punishment for the fall. In relationships, celibacy became the ideal, with sex seen as evil although necessary for procreation. Women were viewed as temptresses and sexist language abounded.

People thus became conscious that the church was non-world, the inauguration of the future kingdom of God. The world was the kingdom of sin. The church and the world were opposed to each other as the redeemed to the unredeemed. Christians lived as strangers in a hostile world. This helped bring clerics and lay Christians together as a people united in opposition to the world. Yet, lack of attention to daily life in the world was ultimately a way of controlling the laity, as the church cared for their salvation but did little to change their world or to help them live their vocation in the world.

Several centuries ago the sense of work as punishment for sin gave rise to the Jansenist praise for work that was difficult, weary, strenuous, and monotonous. Hard work became a way of being faithful to the Lord. This led to the "Protestant Work Ethic" familiar in the U.S., which stressed activity, industry, frugality, and efficiency as religious ideals and portrayed poverty as sin. Many view their work as mere drudgery and a means of survival, which tends to alienate the worker from the results of labor.

We have a secularized version of the Protestant Work Ethic today. We glorify success, preach sacrifice to get ahead, and emphasize individual accomplishments. Work is a way for us to demonstrate our worth. This thinking promotes workaholism and worship of our work. Identifying our worth with our work takes workers away from their families and makes it hard for many persons to accept retirement, unemployment, and disability. Emphasis in our schools and society on work as career stresses marketing one's talents for personal gain, striving to get ahead of others, efficiency as a goal, and competition and power as virtues.

Pope John Paul II reminds us that work is part of our Christian vocation, a way we serve the Lord. When we look at work as a vocation, we strive to use our gifts to create a better world and to serve others. Our focus is on the community, our goal is excellence, and compassion and cooperation are virtues. The dignity of the worker then becomes important, something John Paul II reminds us is lost when capitalism and communism see workers as instruments of production or commodities whose labor is bought like raw materials or energy.

Modern culture degrades work by assigning value to work rather than the worker and by orienting work more and more toward the destruction of life rather than toward creation. One way our culture destroys life is by making us work long hours, not only at our jobs but even at our consumption. Our work and our possessions consume us. We find little time to enjoy life, to build our marriages, to bring children into the world and properly nurture their upbringing, to care for the elderly, or to build healthy communities. Everything becomes work. Controlled by corporate advertisers, television gives us a message of consumption and replaces family, religion, and school as the primary shaper of values. Parishes have increased their professional staffs, especially in areas like social action, while failing to offer a spirituality based on ordinary life in homes and factories.

Work that is ecologically and socially destructive proves very anti-spiritual. Denying the religious meaning of the earth, we then treat it instead as a dead object to be plundered at will. Such work likewise denies the creativity in human labor. Work continues creation, taking raw nature and shaping it to meet human needs, e.g., through medicine. Dorothy Day said: "We are co-creators with God by our responsible acts, whether bringing forth children, producing food, furniture or clothing." Work belongs to our very nature as God entrusts us with the work of finishing the unfinished universe.

We fail to recognize the significance of work for several reasons. Those spiritualities which divided Jesus' followers into the higher and holy way (clergy and religious) and the lower and unholy way (laity) fostered misunderstanding. Only those works done by religious elites in the church were considered holy. Other workers, works, and workplaces were secular and unholy. This sacred/profane dualism saw only those who did specifically religious work as having a vocation from God. Religious elites talked about the work of the laity in terms of moral directives for the worker but seldom in terms of spirituality. Pope John Paul II's *Laborem Exercens* departed from this by offering a profound spirituality of work.

Separation of the sacred from the secular fostered a spirituality of transcendence, where to pursue God one had to reach beyond the secular cycles of sexual reproduction, work, and material concerns. Celibacy for the Latin rite clergy came partly from this attempt to transcend secular life. Such a one-sided focus on transcendence failed to celebrate the Creator's intimate and fertile presence in ongoing creation. Traditional spirituality viewed work as a curse for original sin, done "by the sweat of your brow." Work served to keep us from idleness, which was likely to lead us away from God. Mental labor was a higher form and therefore more heavenly than earthy manual labor. Modern spiritualities still tend to alienate work to the public, technological world, while confining spirituality to the private, psychological world detached from society.

A third distortion would identify work with the process of production and consumption. Labor is an object of production, while consumption is necessary to expand production. This model tends to undermine the family and neighborhood, weakening the ability of the community to renew itself. The role of woman is increasingly adapted to the culturally normative male role which has been alienated from the cycles of reproduction. Youth also fit into this process of production and consumption, taking adolescents away from family time and ties. While this reduction comes to us from secular sources, the church's devaluation of work certainly plays a part.

Healing the Crisis of Work

To recover the spiritual depth of work, we need to understand it as part of continuing creation. A spirituality of immanence suggests that work unfolds and heals creation. Then such sins as sexism, inadequate wages, inhuman working conditions, and destruction of the environment become the perversion that tends to block the creativity of work.

Thus we encounter the Creator in and through the creativity of our work. As we work to sustain and transform the world, we experience this earth as unfolding creation and find the profound natural basis for meeting Mystery. The Creator is present in every point and at every moment of the universe's creative drive, including human work.

Work is a fundamentally religious act when humans participate in the divine creativity. Work brings us into a dynamic unity with the Creator, becoming a foundation of worship. A spirituality for the worker will help us find what is holy in our work. When we do make things better, beautiful, useful, healthy, or helpful through our work, we are finding the sacred and the holy. Of course, evil work exits too, as when we pollute, threaten or destroy life, make useless products or provide services people don't need. Workers may be victims of evil work, not the cause. For example, while holy work respects nature, much of our work treats earth as an object to be plundered. So much work is neither purely holy nor purely evil but ambiguous; thus workers have a religious obligation to try to transform degrading work situations.

Because church leaders fail to affirm the religious aspect of work, we cannot fully blame modern ideologies for doing the same. Contemporary western Christianity has functioned almost entirely on the consumer side of life, relating to members' personal life but rarely to their work experience. Parish workers may visit homes occasionally, but seldom visit workplaces.

To heal the modern degradation of work, we need to see it as profoundly spiritual. In the Old Testament, the real crown of creation is not humanity but the sabbath, which reminds us that creation is God-centered. Genesis sees humans assigned to cherish and care for God's creation. When work lost its harmony through sin, humans were alienated in their ecological, social and spiritual relationships. Sexuality, linked intimately to work in co-creation, also lost its harmony through patriarchal domination and violence. As modern technologies remove us even more from participation in nature, sin's destructiveness also escalates. God is no longer celebrated within the creative process of work, but transcendently remote and accessible only through sacrifices offered by an increasingly separated priesthood, who direct their highest energies toward transcending nature through contemplation of divine realities.

Fortunately, most current spiritual renewal embraces the world. New feminist spiritualities confront the hierarchical dualisms and explore a holistic spirituality of creative embodiment. Creation-centered spirituality integrates the sense of an imminent God with mystical insights emerging from our new scientific awareness. John Paul II focuses Catholic social thought on the co-creativity of work, noting how work unites people, builds up the human community, and allows persons to become fully human by sharing in the divinely driven creativity.

Work relates us to society and to other workers. Work should bring us together to make this world a better place. Love motivates the worker to use his or her talents in faithful and loving service within the community. A spirituality of work asks us to look at what relationships we are building through our work, both in the workplace and at home. When we do build life-giving relationships, show compassion or serve others, we are finding potential holiness in our work. When we are exploitive or use other people, including our family, for our own ends, we fail our Christian calling.

Precious Time

For many hard-working Americans, leisure now means little more than an ever more furious orgy of consumption. We spend whatever energies are left after working in pursuing pleasure, with the help of an endless array of goods and services. Advertisers encourage our leisure time pursuits as a way to consume the products of our work.

Classical spiritualities fostered a destructive attitude toward leisure. Augustine thought that the Christian gave up leisure. Many Americans, growing up with the notion that "idleness is the devil's workshop," work at leisure by being busybodies. If we have a leisure ethic, it is certainly based on the Protestant Work Ethic's sense of activity.

In contrast, John Paul II stresses the need for leisure in his encylical on human labor. The U.S. Bishops' pastoral, *Economic Justice for All*, reminds us: "Leisure is connected to the whole of one's value system. . . . For disciples of Christ, the use of leisure may demand being counter-cultural. The Christian tradition sees in leisure time to build family and societal relationships and an opportunity for communal prayer and worship, for relaxed contemplation and enjoyment of God's creation, and for cultivation of the arts, which help fill the human longing for wholeness" (338).

Leisure as free time is a fairly recent idea. The older meaning of leisure is contemplation – an attitude of peace, centeredness, and wholeness. In leisure, we affirm God as the source and purpose of our existence. Persons who take the same attitude toward leisure as toward work do not value rest and contemplation.

A growing emphasis on self-growth, on relationships with others and with the world around us, brings us closer to the meaning of leisure than does pleasure-oriented consumption. At a time when work tends to depersonalize people, leisure can help us discover ourselves as persons and recover the meaning of life.

Leisure is essentially spiritual. It is a quality of life rather than a period of time. A contemplative person is one who is able to taste, see, feel and hear the Divine Presence in the surrounding world and not outside it. We can find spiritual meaning in the beauty of autumn leaves, a good visit with a friend, or a backyard circus. Properly reflected upon, these natural joys and daily life events are prayerful experiences which ultimately lead us to God.

Leisure is a time for building relationships. Most families recognize the need for a more leisured lifestyle. What we take time for reveals our priorities. The home should be a place where everyone gets attention and time to be appreciated. Family members feel a need to be close. With mothers working and youth busy with work and sports, families do not share much in common. A game, a walk or a ride together allows for casual conversation so essential for love. Giving time is our best gift, the gift of self.

Most people do not take enough time in their busy lives to be with God in celebration and contemplation. Yet being with God is as central to being a Christian as being with spouse and family is central to a married person's life. When we do not have time for contemplation, our image of God hardens, we begin to lose the sense of mystery, and God ceases to be relevant to our daily life. Liturgy and prayer need leisure. Celebration means time to build community, to know and enjoy each other. Both the family meal and the Eucharistic meal need time for sharing and appreciating. Meals are sacred moments.

We need as well to recover the holiness of public life. John Paul II tells us that "Christians have a right and a duty to contribute as far as possible to building up of society." He believes one cannot be a good Christian without being a good citizen. Yet American Catholics, busy with personal salvation, often question whether religion and public life can mix. Groups like the Moral Majority remind us that religion is public rather than private.

Every Christian is gifted by God to participate in the public life of the community. However, the church competes for members' time in church work more often than it encourages parishioners to serve in civic organizations. Growing individualism, plus a feeling of being powerless in the face of corruption in government, nuclear dangers, growing crime, and economic despair, have destroyed the will of many to work for the common good. Yet we see people joining forces to make existing institutions accountable and to gain control over decisions which affect their lives.

Modern church teachings stress commitment to work for a better world as intrinsic to one's vocation. Holiness thus has a social dimension. The U.S bishops' pastoral letters on nuclear warfare and on the economy take the institutional church into the center of American public life. They acknowledge a role for the church in moving society in a healthier direction. Unfortunately, in its efforts to move into social ministry, the church tends to respond primarily to issues that highlight its own needs and interests rather than help members get involved in already established ministries of the civic community.

In *The Challenge of Peace*, the U.S. bishops affirmed the virtue of patriotism. Genuine patriotism has three main elements. One is a love and humanist concern for the people of our country; for the health, happiness, and well-being of all, including the poorest, most deprived, and powerless. Another is a deep reverence for our land, our waters, our air, the environment in which we live, work and play. Finally, there is a commitment to our ideals of freedom and social justice, embodied in such visions as the Declaration of Independence's assurance that all persons are created equal and possess inalienable rights or Abraham Lincoln's concept of a "government of the people, by the people, for the people."

If Christians are to play a role in renewing public life, the church must help us understand how public life relates to the core of our faith. It is not enough to decry evil and unfair public policy without being involved in shaping the civic community. A theology of public life must help us find new ways to live and act together. Too often we form community as a reaction to the brokenness of our society rather than in response to our unity. Communities of retreat rather than engagement and change threaten public life. The role of the community is to draw us out of ourselves into the common life. Contrary to a spirituality which turned us inward, contemplation can serve to clarify our action and action can bear the fruits of contemplation.

Pastoral Implications

In *Economic Justice for All*, the U.S. bishops' stated: "The road to holiness for most of us lies in our secular vocations. We need a spirituality which calls forth and supports lay initiative and witness not just in our churches but also in business, in the labor movement, in the professions, in education and public life. Our faith is not just a weekend obligation, a mystery to be celebrated around the altar on Sunday. It is a pervasive reality to be practiced every day in homes, offices, factories, schools and businesses across our land. We cannot separate what we believe from how we act in the marketplace and the broader community" (25).

Many Catholics who go to work and raise families also search deeply in their spiritual journey. They get little support from the parish and institutional church to guide this search to integrate their work, family life, personal life, and church life. They are looking for others who understand and want to share their effort to focus spirituality on this world rather than on otherworldly concerns.

What does all this mean for the pastoral life of the local church? The starting point is consciousness of the spiritual depth of work and family life. As simple as that sounds, I see little evidence of such awareness. I hinted earlier at reasons for this. Church professionals, who taught spirituality, considered only work done directly for the church institution as religious. Removed from the daily life of the family and secular workplace, they rarely talked about the vocations of marriage and work. Children are amazed to hear pastoral staffs say their parents' work is holy.

Another reason stems from our modern lifestyle. Prior to the Industrial Revolution, production and reproduction were closely connected. Couples and children worked together on the family farm or in the family shop. The Industrial Revolution began the process of separating production from reproduction and work from the family. Today, the physical distance between work and family effectively separates these two realities. Most children cannot relate to what their parents do at work.

The church, meanwhile, established its pastoral response where people lived rather than with reference to the workplace. Pastoral planning has neglected the productive side of work. Robert Bellah notes that even the small Christian faith communities reinforce this split, forming "life-style enclaves" disconnected from members' work. Church themes focus primarily on personal growth and intimate relationships, leaving the area of work outside pastoral and spiritual consciousness.

American Catholics' early experience was different. The church was heavily involved in workers' efforts to find work and to form labor unions. Ethnic ghettos effectively protected workers from the new and hostile industrial society. Today, with large numbers of women and teenagers drawn into the workforce, we tend to fragment our lives into compartments of work, family time, leisure, volunteeer time, and church time. Thus we separate God's time from work and family, easily maintaining an active church life unrelated to our daily activities.

Our pastoral response needs to reflect the family in American culture. We no longer have families where Dad works away from home, mother is home with the children, and the structure is patriarchal. The parish can no longer depend upon women at home to volunteer for the religious education of children. Instead, we see men taking on partnership roles with women in marriage and parenting, with enormous strains leading to epidemic levels of divorce and single parent families. Parish-centered religious socialization separated from the family continues to have a declining influence.

The family and the parish are not insulated from but greatly impacted by the great changes occuring in a technological society that erodes the ecological, social and spiritual realms of our lives. The value system of modern work undermines family, community and parish life. The shifting roles of men and women diminish the religious meaning of traditional spiritualities based on division of these roles.

We face a challenge to create a new model of family based on a male/female partnership in the productive and reproductive spheres as women move into the workforce and men are more involved in family and community. This suggests a new male/female partnership model for the family, for work, and for the church.

Thus far we have not developed a holistic model for this integration of male-female roles. The traditional male domination over the female has been exposed, but our efforts to solve it by democratizing women into the male role have allowed production to erode reproduction.

A spirituality of ordinary holiness regains the religious meaning of sexuality and of work as participating in and continuing God's holy creation. Sex and work are too precious to be left to the secular world devoid of religious meaning. The 1985 Synod called for a spirituality to help the laity "perform their role in the church in their daily occupations such as the family, the workplace, secular activities and leisure time so as to permeate and transform the world with the light of Christ." An incarnational spirituality must discern the presence and movement of God in our daily activities and in each other, in making love and in loving labors as readily as at Sunday Mass.

Since life itself is holy, this spirituality must be based on a love, defense, and celebration of all life, from the embryo to the planet, especially in the way we give life to each other through loving relationships. Seeing our work as participation in God's creation, we need to reshape the world of work and economy to overcome what is dehumanizing, devalues or destroys life, alienates or separates. Our consumer mentality raises questions about stewardship of resources and idolatry of things. Individual actions of resistance are important, as when a young unmarried woman chooses to give life to her child, a college student takes a lower paying job in a nursing home, a parent makes simple toys for Christmas, or a grandmother listens to and befriends the young.

"My contention," says Bishop Albert Ottenweller, "is that right now, organizationally, parishes are very heavy on institution and very light on community. We think institution. We think program. We think service."* The way the local church organizes its common life says far more about the way if believes than all it teaches and preaches. People are far more comfortable with beliefs, rituals, and activities than with relationships. The parish issues a call to belong through a very special relationship among those who share Jesus' mission. This relationship is to form a whole way of life, as alive on Monday as on Sunday. Members are brothers and sisters just as much in the homes, on the streets, in the neighborhood, and on the job as at Sunday Mass. Ideally, it is not the role of the parish to give life to the people. Rather, people who have found life elsewhere give life to the parish.

The familiar parish structure reflected a basically stable society where people lived and worked, were educated and entertained in the same place. In America, the parish became the strong community of the church. Masses of immigrant Catholics huddled in city ghettos, where the parish helped preserve their nationality and their religion. The parish offered a secure haven until Catholics began to move into the mainstream of society.

Today the parish is a structure almost unrelated to those places where people live their lives and where decisions are made in the community. The church is no longer a socializing institution for a more affluent people who feel very little need

---

* Bishop Albert Ottenweller, "Parish Renewal, A Process, Not a Program," *Origins*, Vol. 8, No. 42, (April 5, 1979), pp. 672ff.

for the church in daily living. It is easier for the parish to provide services than to develop a people with a sense of common life and mission. Leaders get so concerned with preparation for liturgies, fund raising, lay ministries, committee meetings and building maintenance that they have little time or energy to prepare members for their vocation. This led Bill Diehl to ask: "How can an organization which spends 99% of its time and energy in maintaining an institution possibly expect that, during a one hour worship service, its people will come to know that their real purpose is to be spending ninety-nine percent of their time as God's agents of love and reconciliation in the world?"*

People look outside the parish today for many functions it once provided or shop around for a parish that meets their needs. They make a conscious choice about how they will participate in church life. Pastoral ministers need to remind themselves that community life exists to support the mission of the church, since they are tempted in their busyness to invert this priority. Most parish renewal is focused on developing ministries within the parish, even though work and family shape people's identity and social relationships. The church lives in our homes, offices, factories, and legislative halls. If it does not live there, then it cannot live in the buildings we call churches.

Actions to Consider

• This chapter deals with some of our most basic paradigms, the lens through which we see our world. Family-centered persons get their security and personal worth from family traditions and are vulnerable to major changes in family life. Because work-centered persons get their identity and sense of self worth from their work, they are vulnerable to anything that keeps them from continuing it. Here we deal with people's vision and values.

• How can we reintegrate work and family life back into religious consciousness and pastoral strategy? A good place to begin lies with liturgy and preaching. The Sunday liturgy

---

* William E. Diehl, *Thank God, It's Monday* (Philadephia: Fortess Press, 1982), p. 90.

should be the place where we celebrate the religious meaning of life during the week. Unfortunately, we now bring very little of people's life experiences into the liturgy. Our starting point might be to simply acknowledge the religious depth of work, family life, and public service.

• Pastoral workers ought to be well acquainted with life in the homes and workplaces. They might provide opportunities to discuss and reflect on the religious aspects of these experiences. Before long, liturgical and pastoral responses would reflect the holiness of ordinary life.

• Pastoral ministers who try to embrace a partnership model of family and work, of production and reproduction, need to find new ways to minister to spouses and families. They might advocate less emphasis on work and a shortened work week so spouses have more time for each other, for children, for community, and for parish life. They might assign someone to minister on family/work issues, or form support groups to help families sort out their questions. To continue with ministry as is likely means the loss of many female workers and whole families to the church.

• Unemployment is a religious issue because it denies persons the right to be co-creators with the rest of society. In *Laborem Exercens,* John Paul II reaffirmed the need for labor unions as an indispensible element of industrial life. Workers deserve some decision-making power within the workplace. That means the Christian community cannot be neutral on the rights of labor anymore than it can be neutral on the rights of the unborn. We might shed our present dualism if we recognized those persons who do "holy work" at the workplace as readily as those involved in church ministry.

• The U.S. Bishops remind us that leisure is a "time to build family and societal relationships and an opportunity for communal prayer and worship, for relaxed contemplation and enjoyment of God's creation, and for cultivation of the arts. . . ." How about some homilies on the meaning of leisure in our lives? Model this by taking the time for silence and reflection in parish liturgies, which are too busy with words rather than contemplation and community building as we share a meal together. The church faces a real challenge today to convince people they need quiet time for prayer and reflection in their cluttered lives.

• Celebrations like Holy Thursday offer a chance to give footwashing awards to persons who minister apart from the parish liturgy. Persons who serve in volunteerism and community service, as well as those who minister at work and at home, will be surprised when the parish acknowledges the value and significance of their daily lives.

6

The Grace
of Sexual Communion

> You carry out the mission of the home in ordinary
> ways when you foster intimacy, beginning with the
> phyical and spiritual union of the spouses, and ex-
> tending in appropriate ways to the whole family.

REDBOOK MAGAZINE SURPRISED A LOT OF AMERICANS A FEW YEARS
ago with a study relating the connection between women's
sexuality and religion. A headline announcing this study in
the *Minneapolis Star Tribune* read: "Religious Women More
Sexually Satisfied." *Redbook* found that the more religious a
woman was, the more she enjoyed sexual lovemaking, the
more she initiated it, and the more frequently she and her husband had sexual relations.

This study holds a powerful message for the church and
for family ministers. We have changed our paradigms regarding married sexuality, but we still seem unable to grasp how
sexuality relates to spirituality. For centuries the church's
teaching was influenced by Gnosticism and Jansenism, which
connected sexuality with the material world and considered it
opposed to the spiritual realm. Most early Christian writers
believed the problem with sex was that it was so pleasurable it
overrode reason, weakened the resolution of the will, and led
people into sin. Augustine insisted that even marital sex for
procreation was at least venially sinful because it was so impossible to experience sex without pleasure.

Western spirituality was generally involved in a flight
from sensuality. It placed the business of saving souls over
inspiring persons to love life and to share it. The church often

encouraged abstinence for spouses, e.g., a manual for Catholic priests used in America until a few years ago directed the priest to advise a married couple that if they wanted communion on Sunday morning they should abstain from sexual relations Saturday night. Where was the sense that communion signified the unity of God's people, a unity also expressed by a sacramental couple's lovemaking? The fear of passion neglected the balance with compassion, i.e., sharing the pleasure as well as enjoying the pleasure.

We entered the twentieth century understanding sex primarily for procreation. The 1917 Code of Canon Law and Pius XI's *Casti Connubi* described the mutual help spouses gave one another as a secondary but nonessential good of the marriage relationship. Even Vatican II viewed procreation as the main purpose of marriage: "Marriage and conjugal love are by their nature ordained toward begetting and educating children. Children are really the supreme gift of marriage and contribute very substantially to the welfare of their parents. The God Himself who said 'It is not good for man to be alone' (Gen. 2:18) and who 'made man from the beginning male and female' (Mark 19:4) wished to share with man a certain participation in his own creative work. Thus he blessed male and female, saying: 'Increase and multiply.'"*

Vatican II did affirm that sex could help a couple to grow in their love relationship. Thus it acknowledged the two purposes of lovemaking as procreation and the expression of mutual love. *We have yet to create an active paradigm truly integrating the spiritual dimension of sex.* Perhaps the barrier comes in treating sex from a pathological stance more often than as a gift from God, something we do rather than an expression of who we are and what we mean to each other. Thus we control sexual behavior through rules focused more on avoidance of sexual sin and a bias in favor of celibacy than by affirming the beauty of our sexuality.

Unfortunately, advertisers have proclaimed sex as the savior of the day. Sex has been elevated to the key human experience without a spiritual understanding. The results are drastic. Sex is no longer understood in the context of perma-

---

* *Gaudium et Spes*, 50.

nent relationships and severed from fertility. Sex as personal pleasure is seen as an end in itself. Cut off from emotional risk-taking and severed from the potent possibility of creating life, sex has been gutted of symbolic meaning.

Meanwhile, the institutional church has spent much energy to protect the ethic allowing sex to be enjoyed only in marriage and with openness to the procreation of children. American Catholics have drastically changed their attitudes toward premarital sex and the rules governing sexual conduct in marriage. For example, Andrew Greeley reports in his surveys that nine out of ten American Catholics do not believe birth control is wrong, and only 17% of American Catholics believe premarital sex is always wrong. While moral theology is not determined by people's attitudes and behavior, these statistics raise questions about how well both the church's teachers and the people of God understand sex. Better understanding might have tempered today's phenomenon of cohabitation, where the church has been largely silent toward a practice proving very destructive of marital stability.

Two-thirds of recent marriages were preceded by cohabitation despite all the evidence that living together before marriage is not a good choice. Premarital sex trivializes one of God's greatest gifts and the commitment of marriage. A sex for pleasure mentality certainly plays into this, although experts see the breakdown of family life as the proximate cause for the popularity of cohabitation. A church serious about reversing the cohabitation trend should nourish and support family life.

The 1960s debate over contraception convinced many lay Catholics that the clerics to whom they turned for help with their decisions had a very different approach to sexuality than did married couples. Many married couples find their experiences of sex and its role in marriage seems contrary to the dominant treatment of sex in church tradition. Catholics have obviously rejected the church's right to dictate on sexual matters, asking the church to stay out of their bedroom, while church leaders try to preserve the Catholic sexual ethic by authority. If these leaders had led a dialogue in search for the meaning of sexuality rather than laying down the law, their credibility might have endured. Instead, priests accused the

Catholic laity of following a worldly and presumed pagan morality more often than they or Catholic documents affirmed the holiness of sexuality.

Had the church entered a dialogue with married couples, it might have found ways to help people understand their curiousity about the human body before they learned to frown at it, moralize about it, and abstact it away into sin. We have tried to tame the erotic within us rather than welcome the creaturely side of human nature and understand sexuality as also taking pleasure in the mysterious. Consequently, the spirits we fail to name and embrace within ourselves manifest themselves in unhealthy if not abusive ways.

The guilt people tend to overidentify with sexuality is not in fact a guilt for being sexual, because we were made that way, but a guilt that comes from living and loving the sensual way we were made. Many couples who appreciate sex feel they should value the companionship, comfort, and intimate bonding they experience in sex and not the physical pleasure, which somehow seems un-Christian. Yet ecstasies are both sensual and spiritual experiences. Blessing is the biblical word for pleasure. The ecstasies of creation are primal sacraments meant to seal our experience of the divine.

Certainly the negative sexual teachings of the Catholic church interfere with the marital pleasures of Catholic spouses. In the 1970s, the Pontifical Commission on the Family warned husbands and wives to be aware of the risks of "unbridled lust" in their relationship. Even though John Paul II recognizes the potential for marital sex, he emphasizes restraint rather than passion. Papal encyclicals and church instructions, however, likely have not had a major effect because Catholics lack familiarity with them.

Families, neighbors and friends, who passed along more of the Catholic tradition, have viewed the passion between husbands and wives much more tolerantly. Catholicism recognizes the sacramental aspect of sexuality and celebrates it in rituals, art, music, and the stories of ordinary people. The wedding ritual states: "The love of man and woman is made holy in the sacrament of matrimony and becomes the mirror of your everlasting love" (Preface #3). Many happily married couples can relate sex with grace. In the past, when marriage beds were blessed to hallow the sexual love between the bride and groom, no one thought it strange.

The relationship that emerges from sex in marriage is dependent upon sex being pleasurable to create intimacy and bonding. Love is not something abstract but a relationship with a real flesh and blood person. Many persons find the experience of orgasm in loving marriage the clearest experience of the divine they have ever known. In this orgasmic experience they feel known and loved in the depth of their souls, free to let go of their very consciousness and become totally vulnerable to the loved one. This mirrors the optimal relationship with God.

Good, frequent and mutually pleasurable sex is as vital to the vocation of marriage as reception of Eucharist is to membership in the church community. In *Familiaris Consortio,* John Paul II said married laity, in virtue of the charism of the sacrament of matrimony, have a unique and indispensable contribution to make to the church's understanding of sexual morality. Unfortunately, we have yet to deepen the dialogue between church leadership, theologians and married couples.

Sacramental Sexuality

Might we build a paradigm for sexuality on the Song of Songs, which sees sexual love to be a hint of the divine love? Falling in love is an exhilarating experience that preocuppies and fills a person with sexual longing that makes one's whole life both glorious and exhausting. For many people, sex is certainly the most powerful and moving experience life has to offer and more overwhelmingly holy than anything that happens in church. In the mixture of familiarity and mystery, falling in love again with a spouse is perhaps the most intense erotic experience in the human condition. Catholic tradition sees a correlation between the ecstasy of rediscovering and being rediscovered physically and emotionally by the intimate other with being discovered by the Other. Religious imagery, symbolism and behavior are intimately connected to romance.

If God is near and vitally present in all of life, then we see why ecstasy is the experience of God. The giver is present in the gifts in an extraordinary, intimate way. To experience such natural ecstasies as sex deeply, to the extent of forgetting oneself in this pleasure, is to experience the object of faith, the Gift-giver. Sexual loving is central to the vocation of marriage. Without the sexual exchange of love and grace, a relationship is not marital.

The *Redbook* study hints that the greatest payoff in romance comes from a mixture of religion or religious images and frequent sex. Our image of God has an important effect on romantic love. Those who see God as a lover, a spouse, a friend and a mother are twice as likely to say they are in the romance or falling in love stage as those who see God as a judge, master and father, according to Andrew Greeley.* The American church presented a judgmental God, who considered sexual sins the most "mortal."

The interaction between the religious and the erotic is intricate. Couples who knew the excitment of passion in their early marriage find that intimate play actually increases with age for those who are in love and diminishes for those who are not. Psychologists give us the Marital Intimacy Scale, which says that the quality of a couple's sexual relationship depends largely on the quality of their total relationship, which depends upon the quality of their communication, which in turn depends largely on the quality of their openness and listening. A couple wishing to improve their sexual life, then, had best work on their openness and listening skills rather than pursuing new positions and techniques as a panacea. Actually, the face is our most important sexual organ because it effectively conveys our feelings and responses.

Sex is a powerful outward symbol of the inner temper of a marital relationship. In reality, the quality of a marriage in all of its facets depends upon a wholesome and satisfying sex life. Likewise, partners' feelings about marriage as a whole will almost always be reflected in the quality of their sexual life. Some people find it hard to admit that the body plays such a preeminent role in the spiritual life. While sex is not the only aspect of a physical relationship in marriage, most

---

* Andrew Greeley, "Sex and the Married Catholic: The Shadow of St. Augustine," *America*, Vol. 167, No. 13, (October 31, 1992), p. 318ff.

often it is the touchstone for responses and sacrifices made for each other.

Although the church focused spirituality on a monastic model and never had a well-developed spirituality for spouses, married life is a spiritual life, a life of holiness. A married person's holiness does not come in spite of marriage but through response to this call to love. Each sacrament has a particular symbol that signifies the grace it causes, and that symbol for marriage is the love life of the couple properly united in sexual intimacy. The church hinted at this by requiring that a marriage be consummated sexually to be a valid sacramental union. Sexual intercourse draws the couple into a life with God. Married holiness flows especially from intimacy based on the kind of love that culminates in sexual intercourse. A married spirituality, then, would focus on deepening the couple's sexual intimacy.

Sexuality is God's gift calling us out of our aloneness into relationship. We are born as incomplete individuals, with a loneliness innate to our human existence. The remedy is intimacy, a sharing in other people's lives. In marital intimacy we come into a communion with another person, so that two become one without ceasing to be two. In that spiritual reality, individual identities are not lost but strengthened and enhanced. Any person psychologically or emotionally alienated from his or her sexuality is handicapped in the pursuit of human intimacy.

Spirituality implies wholeness. Our understanding of spirituality has already embraced an intimacy with God. We are called to love God with our whole heart, mind and soul. In that intimacy with God, we share God's ecstatic happiness. But we humans do not expect enough from God, underestimating God's incredible love for us. God also wants us to love others deeply, to build intimate relationships that establish a communion of persons. God allows us the freedom to make this commitment to the divine plan. We can only come to know the God who is love and who loves us unconditionally if we have an experience of loving and being loved simply for who we are. In our love for each other, we provide the experience of human intimacy that makes divine intimacy credible.

Sacraments are symbols that point us to the profound mystery they signify. A symbol begins with an experience that is too big for a single exclamation. Symbols stand for many, though always ecstatic, experiences. One who has been moved responds in symbols. We interpret our experiences through symbols, which communicate messages between people. In making love, we symbolize our unity. Even in a loving marriage, however, spouses can use sex for physical pleasure without the offer of their bodies symbolizing the total gift of self.

Sacraments presume the sensual. The Eucharist is a profoundly sensual event. So is baptism with water, oily consecration of church ministers and anointing of the sick, and sex is marriage. Thomas Aquinas took his basic symbolism for the sacraments from the very physical and sensual life of the human body, such as birth, puberty, eating, injuries, and sexual activity. American Catholicism, with its Jansenistic bias and reaction to the sexual expression of our culture, most often avoids the sensual. We need to once again expect the potential sensuousness of sacraments.

In experiencing ecstasy, we are experiencing what our forefathers in spiritual traditions called "grace." Sacraments give us grace. Just as sacraments are actions, not things, so grace is a relationship with God, not a quality but a shared reality of God's presence. As I said earlier, in the broad range of activity that is sacramental, no doubt the most basic is human love. Sexual intercourse does not just express or symbolize love, it creates love as two persons penetrate each other's body and spirit in an incarnate intimacy. Present to each other as two unique individuals, they long to share that uniqueness with each other in an experience of total oneness of body and spirit.

The shared love of a couple moves naturally to the begetting of a third person. As a couple grow in love for each other, a child takes on greater meaning as an outward expression of their love. They desire to enflesh their love as a gift to each other. God plants this desire in the hearts of a husband and wife so that they incarnate their mutual love in a new person who expresses their ecstatic oneness. The child is a unique gift from God and an extension of themselves. This desire for a third person continues as spouses wish to give the oneness of their love to all other persons they meet in life. An appreciation of procreative sexuality could do a lot to free couples from the tyranny of discontent and the temptation of infidelity.

Sexual Intimacy

If marital sex truly symbolizes marital love, then marital sex becomes a school for love. When spouses bare their total selves, not only their bodies but their feelings, desires, fears and commitments, and offer themselves to a loved spouse who loves them, they are rewarded not only by physical pleasure but with intimacy that offers closeness, communion, and companionship. As spouses learn the rewards of giving themselves fully in sex, they are moved to give themselves to each other in all the other areas of their shared life, trusting their gifts of time, effort and confidence will be returned and multiplied.

Sacramental spouses live in an ongoing state of intimacy. This intimacy is achieved and celebrated in a special way through sexual intercourse. In the shared vulnerability, persons allow a spouse to touch them at the deepest levels of their being, to be changed by the relationship as they know and are known in a unique way. This intimacy is an open sharing of each other's psychological selves, achieved by altruistic love, by a mutual concern and enjoyment of each other's goodness.

If such intimacy of happily married couples is the correct story for marriage, then theology is moving into a territory barely explored by Catholic theologians and authorities. Who else but men and women who have taken down their protective barriers and risked their passion in marriage can say what sexual love may do to take away fear of losing individual privacy and freedom. The church has done little to learn the religious meaning of sexuality from committed and happily married couples. Their experience correlates with a very different kind of sexual and interpersonal life than that reported by most Americans. In fact, the romantic marriage probably represents a form of marital intimacy that most married people think impossible for themselves.

Intimacy is more than sexual lovemaking. Being male or female is not an incidental characteristic. Our sexuality marks every cell of our bodies, as well as our feelings, minds and wills. The sexes are complementary, not just different, and related like two opposite poles attracting each other. Human nature needs to be completed and complemented by some sort of union with a person of the opposite sex. The desire to stay close to the person who gives such deep pleasure is part of the symbolism of sexual intercourse within sacramental marriage. It is how sex creates the love it signifies. John Paul II talks about this as the "nuptial meaning of the body."

In their daily life together, spouses live self-abandoning love culminating in sexual intercourse. The ecstasies of sexual enjoyment constitute an experience beyond oneself, a taste of the divine. At least they can. That kind of ecstasy happens best when it combines the experience of nature and friendship. It culminates in compassion, an awareness of the integral relationship between one's own and others' ecstasies. The commandment for persons committed to the experience of ecstasy is pleasure first, not only one's own pleasure but also another's pleasure, the way God does with us. We act out the same kind of passionate, self-abandoning love when we do what is appropriate in our contact with other people.

One certain criterion for a spiritual sensuality will be its sharing dimension. In this way, marriage sets the norm for Catholic spiritual life. The mystics trying to describe intimacy with God do so in the language of married love, of sexual intimacy. Spiritual does not mean withdrawl from the world or from the pleasure of our bodies, but life embued with divine presence. This life has always been deeply incarnational, not a life of flight from our bodies.

For all of us, married and celibate, holiness comes through a love that is humanly whole, which involves our bodies, our emotions, and our sexuality. To love someone looks to the good of the other person rather than seeking to fulfill our own needs. Love asks "What can I do for you?" or "Who can I be for you?" We identify the other person's happiness as our own, because we love our beloved as our other self.

The nature of love decides the quality of intimacy. We need not lose anything of our own when we enter into communion with another unique person. As that person comes into our mind and heart, we grow even through ours is a simple decision to care for another. When we see our beloved, we feel more than sexual urgings; we feel a reverence. When spouses enjoy such intimacy, enacted in genital sex, our love becomes a sacrament leading us to intimacy with our Creator. However, the divine aspect of sexuality seldom arises unless we first turn inward and integrate our sexual being into the total pattern of our lives. Sexuality rarely brings us to the fullness of love and wholeness, to an experience of God, unless we have a conscious spiritual life and a growing relationship with God into which we integrate it.

Since sacramental symbols cause what they signify, their accuracy is very important. That which is specific to matrimony is sexual ecstasy. What is there about sexual intercourse which makes it an epitome of marital intimacy? When intercourse is an enactment of love that produces intimacy, orgasm is a moment of supreme generosity, of an intimacy that is as complete as it can be. Any loving action requires some degree of self-abandonment. In the moment of orgasm, the last shred of self-consciousness is gone for at least one ecstatic moment. We lovingly abandon our whole self, body, mind and heart, into the hands of the one we love, as completely as we can. Sexual intercourse, then, is the powerful body language of passionate, altruistic communion that such love produces.

Thus, there is good reason why the church affirms sexual intercourse as central to the sacramental symbol of marriage. In no other human action do persons so dramatically give themselves to each other and thus become totally themselves. Their desire for unity is simultaneously a desire to be in union with the life of God in them. Intercourse is not merely a symbol, but an effective cause of a loving way of life that causes spouses to be drawn into the inner life of God.

When sexual lovemaking becomes the usual way couples express their love for each other, it easily becomes irritating and frustrating. Sacramental sexuality must be an enactment of mutual, generous, self-sacrificing concern. When couples embrace the common hierarchical model of a dominant husband and a subordinate wife, a power imbalance makes communication difficult. This invites dependency more than the trust needed for intimacy. We trust because we love, not because of obligations. Satisfying sex presupposes equality. Tender concern and self-abandonment must mark all the trivial and profound daily encounters that gradually weave the web of a couple's intimacy.

Most of us have a hard time accepting sexual desires as good. We have too long identified these desires as, if not shameful, at least selfish. It seems sex has to be purified before it can become sacramental. Yet we experience people as most unselfish when they are in love and feel a strong sexual desire for each other. The attraction for each other is deep within and turns us from the natural focus on ourselves to be preoccupied with another. This attraction is not something we plan or make happen. Sexual attraction is the grace of vocation.

In the mystery of growing together, spouses find that in putting another's fulfillment ahead of their own, they are fulfilled. In the sacrament of matrimony, we discover that in losing our life by giving it to another, we find our life, in and with our spouse. In transcending the exclusive boundaries of self through sexual intimacy, we find that repeatedly answering the call of sexual desire leads to ecstatic abandonment of self to another that brings us to a fulfilling communion.

The Hebraic image of God and Israel making love together harbors profound truth. Perhaps it is a hint, even a revelation, of our relationship with the pleasure-loving, pleasure-providing Creator. Who dares to measure what God's pleasures might be, having tasted the depth of natural ecstasies? In the process of being reborn by ecstatic experiences, we are to some degree remade. Thus, when we spend time with the ecstasies of creation, including sexual lovemaking, we become like the Creator and take on the Creator's characteristics. We recover what it means to be "made in the image and likeness of God."

Hanging Onto Sexual Intimacy

Marriages go through cycles. In the romance stage, sexual desires are high. When romance fades, some find the courage to renew their romance under the impetus of sexual desire. But they may soon find themselves back in disillusionment or misery. Couples with struggling relationships often avoid sex or use each other for sexual pleasure. If sexual passion is a sacramental cause of grace, a God-given gift for healing selfishness, why isn't it more attractive? Even couples who try to be more attentive to each other and to spend time together frequently find themselves in an emotional desert with only an occasional sexual oasis. They lose the sexual urgency that constitutes their basic identities as husband and wife and come to be more friends than lovers, living together and meeting their responsibilities. Their life is no longer marked by that sexual passion that forms the core of the sacrament of matrimony.

Many couples in the cycle of settling down or disillusionment may have intercourse frequently enough, but the total union of persons is lacking. The total awareness of each other as sexually desired and loved fades. Sex becomes an activity they do rather than the aura in which they do everything. They are no longer the center of each other's attention. They are not tied together by the bond of sexual desire. They may feel important to each other, and make many sacrifices for each other, but their marriage is not their source of energy.

In a truly sacramental marriage, spouses do not see themselves as married singles but as utterly and joyously given over to each other. That kind of self-abandon is not possible without a continuously cultivated sexual passion. They are tied to each other by a promise to be sexually present to each other all the days of their lives. To neglect their sexual passion is a genuine infidelity to each other, the marring of the sacramental symbol.

Sexual passion, then, is not one compartment of marriage, an area apart from the whole relationship, but the total aura of life as spouses. Sexual love is not one of the things a couple do together, like fixing meals or raising children. If it is, they learn to use sex to manipulate each other, give sex as a reward, withhold it as punishment, and try new techniques to make it exciting when it gets boring. No doubt all the excuses for rejecting sexual lovemaking, such as too tired, headaches, not the right time, or we'll wake the children could be summed up in one reason, namely, not in the mood. That mood changes when everything a couple does is colored by desire for each other.

Seeing themselves as private persons is a real tragedy, which often leads spouses to find a third person to fill up loneliness or to fall in love with their work or hobbies. Putting oneself first mars and obscures the symbolism of their life of generous vowed love, thus inhibiting the power of the sacrament to cause what it signifies. This weakened ability to love each other leads to inhibited intimacy with each other and with the God who lives in them. Efforts to cultivate passion in marriage are thus likely a matter of life or death for the relationship. The conflict between maintaining sexual desire and allowing it to atrophy is really a conflict between egoism and altruism, between selfishness and love. Our spiritual life is basically about losing our life in order to find it.

The sacramental life of a couple creates a sexual aura in their home and in their entire lives. Whether physically present to each other or not, they are in each other's minds and hearts by a sexual awareness and desire. They are not preoccupied with unforgiven hurts or fearful of future demands from each other, and the lines of separation between them grow ever weaker. This sexual desire is a healing, redemptive, God-given grace.

To place the cultivation of sexual passion at the heart of married spirituality may seem irrelevant or blasphemous. We have not yet moved far enough beyond the sense of sex as evil to allow ourselves to freely become sensual bodies (incarnate). Some people find the notion of a relationship between spirituality and sexuality shocking. We make our spirituality otherworldly, being used to a sense of warring against sexuality as evil. However, couples do not find their spirituality primarily in prayer and frequent attendance at Mass. Sexual passion is truly the basis of their spirituality. A couple who make the most of their sexual desire, especially those who reflect the power of regular and satisfying lovemaking over years of marriage, are the clearest symbol of the love God calls us to in belonging to each other. They become bone of each other's bones and flesh of each other's flesh. In order to love God passionately, we also have to be a passionate, sexual person.

Is it realistic to think that couples can stay passionately excited about each other? Yes! That aura exists among the engaged and can be maintained if given first priority. Perhaps the ultimate test of a couple's love lies in whether or not they can believe in and build on those times of almost perfect giving and acceptance, never doubting or resenting or forgetting these holy times afterwards in the stress and trial of daily life. Those who perceive themselves to be in love are more likely to pray together and to enjoy an intense erotic life. Praying together and playing together does, indeed, account for husband and wife being more likely to stay together. Ultimately the pleasure a couple experience is not theirs alone but their neighbors' as well. This is the best gift a couple can give their children and the community.

One great challenge for the church is to help people understand the symbolic centrality of sex to marriage. Our culture is influenced by and hungry for symbolism and the meaning and values it conveys, but also disdains our symbols and is ready to reject the symbols inherited from the past. We need to be concerned about how spouses perceive their identities and how that perception motivates their daily choices. Without the sexual aura that comes from making each other the center of their lives, couples fail to show the distinctively marital quality. One way to help them foster and cherish the passion that first brought them together is to enable healthy communication, the deep and honest sharing of inward thoughts and feelings which is culminated in the epitome of intimate body language, sexual intercourse.

Primary responsibility for sex education falls on the family-centered church. To be able to talk to their children openly about sex in marriage, parents must first be able to communicate with each other about sex in their marriage. What children need most from their parents is a sense of how a sexual relationship functions. They want to know that their parents are loving and appreciate each other physically.

Marriage is founded on the community of faith. The community bears a responsibility toward each couple called to be a sacrament of the church. Marital intimacy needs to be nurtured and enriched by a broader communal covenant with the Lord. In that bonding by which the intimacy of a couple sustains and is sustained by the larger community, we see the connection between the church as the basic sacrament of Christ and matrimony as the primary call to build a faith community. Such a bonding is countercultural, however. It views marriage not as a contract based on power, but as a covenant based on love.

Thus, a major task of the community should be aimed at fostering sexual intimacy in couples. We not only celebrate this love in the wedding ceremony, where we might ritualize the sexual dimension better, but have a stake in a couple's sexual love. We cannot in good conscience surrender this area to the secular sex therapists, as it is too central to the sacrament of matrimony. Many troubled marriages could be helped without counselors if couples would learn to communicate openly with each other, especially about marital sex, where communication is so lacking that even small problems can destroy the relationship.

This calls for an entirely different approach to how we foster marital spirituality. This approach of deepening sexual intimacy will at first seem frightening and even anti-Christian to many of the faithful, but deserves to be worked at anyway. Opportunities can be found in support groups, retreats, renewal movements, and certainly in parish homilies. Parents need to hear how they pass along a sense of the sacred to their children through sexual responses that counteract the message mom teaches about sex as she shouts and hides behind the shower curtain when her five year old son walks in on her partially clad in the bathroom. Couples who enjoy a genuine sexual intimacy play a powerful role in building the very community that supports them, the church. The parish church needs them as much as they need the parish.

Who can deny the powerful experience of being present to a couple who obviously enjoy each other sexually and, as a result, are sensitive and forgiving to those they meet? Their sexual intimacy leads to benevolent love for others. They are powerfully transformed as romance deepens with time into unity. The unity of body and soul, of will and feelings, is no place more evident than in the intense feelings of sexual love.

The call to love each other as God loves us includes a sexual, passionate element because we are sexual, passionate beings. We are not spirits trapped in our bodies, seeking to escape to become spiritual. Our bodies, complete with sexual and other passions, are our very selves. Hence, the church should tell us that to give ourselves to our beloved includes the gift of our sexuality and passions and of helping the other person to grow to his or her full self as a sexual and passionate person. Failure to appreciate sexual communion puts marriage at risk.

In a sharing session for engaged couples, I was asked how often a couple should make love in marriage. I said, "Just follow the church's teaching." After a pause, one young man said: "You mean the church has a teaching on that too?" "Of course," I answered, "Catholic couples make love on days beginning with 'T' – Tuesday, Thursday, Triday, Taturday, Today, Tommorow." Another young man quickly concluded: "Father, didn't you forget Tis-morning and Tis-afternoon?" I gave him a gold star. In this time of busy-ness, alienated families, and high divorce, the church would be far richer if couples took more time for sexual intimacy.

Actions to Consider

• Right now the average parish is quite silent on sexual matters. Clergy find it hard to talk about moral issues when many couples disagree with the church. As teacher, the church needs to speak about sexuality, presenting the ideal without simply decrying failure to live up to the ideals. Allowing married couples to share from their experience can be more credible than celibates who cannot share lived experiences.

• Sexual intimacy is so important to marriage that we should take great care to prepare persons to be good lovers of their spouses. Because marriage is a sacrament, much of the responsibility for this preparation falls to the church. Right now our marriage preparation programs do not deal adequately with sexuality. In reality, engaged couples have such poor sexual education that it would be impossible for the church to deal adequately with sexuality before marriage, no matter what the resources. But good couple sharing can help them to understand the role of sexuality in a healthy relationship.

• One way for the church to improve marriage preparation lies in supporting values-oriented sex education programs in schools. Apart from sexual ignorance, the legacy of sexual repression leaves us with few persons who are comfortable teaching about sexuality. Priests are inexperienced and thus not great teachers or counselors. Married couples have little experience and comfort in sharing their sexual activities or the role of sex in marriage. They often are uncomfortable using a sexual vocabulary in groups, let alone trying to describe how sex has functioned in their marriage as a source of grace. Yet the most effective way to communicate is to share our stories.

• It's difficult to know what to do with cohabiting couples who approach the church for marriage. By the time they come to the parish they have decided to marry, which will soon put cohabitation behind them. The message that cohabitation is not a good way to prepare for a stable marriage needs to reach them earlier. Of 100 couples who live together, only about 15 will end up with intact marriages. Our message needs to contradict that of society which says "It's better to try the shoe on before you wear it." We have statistics to prove these couples face almost certain disaster. We try to talk teens out of smoking for their health. Is not speaking up even more important here?

• While the parish affirms the ideal of marital sexual love, we still need to be sensitive to questions such as the lifestyle of homosexual members, sex among the unmarried, including the large number of persons who are single again after divorce or death of a spouse, the wrenching questions surrounding birth control, and all the human struggles to live up to the use of God's gift of sexuality. A positive theology of sex will invite persons to see the spiritual dimension in this gift from God.

7

The Joy of Socks (Matching)

A family is holy not because it is perfect, but because God's grace is at work in it, helping it to set out anew every day on the way of love.

OUR WORLD TODAY EXPERIENCES A GREAT HUNGER FOR SPIRI-tuality, for meaning. Our biggest spiritual ill, boredom, stems from a lack of meaning and meaningful relationships in our lives. When families do look for spirituality, they look most often to the traditional spiritualities and find them sterile or unrelatable. These spiritualities do not fit the life of the family.

Discussing family spirituality in *Familiaris Consortio,* Pope John Paul II includes all kinds of family events. Virtually everything about family life can become important elements in formulating family spirituality. Many struggle with this, con-necting spirituality with very religious things like church attendance, formal prayers or ascetical practices. Genuine spirituality has never been limited to those actions which most people call religious. Spirituality does not make us other-worldly; it renders us more fully alive and grateful for the wonders in and around us that reveal God's presence.

Spirituality has to do with the way we live our daily life. Since those who wrote about the spiritual life were almost all priests or religious celibates, what they wrote about was the daily events of their lives. Thus we had a warped spirituality, out of focus with the life to which God calls most people, one that often perceived sexuality as an obstacle to spirituality and focused on individual piety rather than on relationships and daily concerns. As ordinary families begin to talk about their spirituality, we will develop a new sense of spirituality relatable to the laity. The parish can play a vital role in this search to discover a spirituality for family life. Parish staffs serve as spiritual guides and leaders.

The paradigm shift for family spirituality takes us away from a disembodied, individual, and otherworldly approach to create a spirituality which is embodied, built on relationships, and centered on the holiness of ordinary life. Not primarily about long hours of prayer or daily ascetical practices, it is a spirituality of struggling relationships, dirty laundry, cluttered kitchens, carrying out the garbage, budget shortages, reconciliation, and hanging in there with each other. These moments are as holy as weddings and the family rosary. Lived creatively and with commitment to each other, they make real, i.e., incarnate, God's love for each person.

A spiritual life for the laity, formulated out of the raw material of daily life, will embrace the spirit of family life with all its complexities. It will look beyond the salvation spirituality most of us learned as children to find the holiness in caring for each other's needs, challenging each other's potential, and rebuilding each other's egos. Discussion of family spirituality should not romanticize or idealize family life, which is messy. While warmth, affection and support mark life in the family, so do harsh conflict, raw hurt and horrible indifference. When the family celebrates its "Eucharist," it does so amid the clamor, the confusion, and the messiness of the average family meal.

Nor should spirituality focus on family pathology. So much discussion on family life today deals with brokenness, pain from families of origin, conflict resolution, and divorce. Most of our families are scarred by such problems as lack of communication, quarreling between generations, alcoholism, financial worries, overcommitment, or a search for the elusive happiness promised by consumerism. Yet we look to our homes as the place where we get our identity and as the primary source for nurture. Home is the place where we are rooted. We have an intuitive sense that God's own life can somehow be touched in the faces, places and events of our family life, often finding hope even in the midst of pain. The family needs to know itself as a people who celebrate the gift of life itself and the gift of each individual life.

Family Systems

Each family is unique. Each family itself forms a system, a community of interrelated parts. This may seem like a strange place to start talking about family spirituality, but it is essentially where we must start. In the past, the church approached its ministry primarily from the point of view of the individual rather than of the whole and the relationships that exist between members. When we look at the family as a system, we lift the interaction between the members of the whole to a place of prominence and place less emphasis upon the role of the individual. Obviously, this contrasts with traditional spirituality's focus on the individual seeking to escape this world to be with God. We then can develop a spirituality based on the interrelationship of family members with each other and with God, which Paul seems to have understood well in his images for the body of Christ.

A systems approach to the family is common with counselors. It suggests ways for handling the complexities rather than being overwhelmed by the problems of family life. Family members are never in isolation but part of the community we call the family centered church. They live with Jesus' promise to be present where two or three are gathered in his name, commanded to "Love one another as I have loved you."

Family ministry must absolutely address the dimension of relationship. It is in our families that we learn or fail to learn how to get along with each other and how to communicate or not communicate. A family system constitutes a group of interrelated parts, each responding to the other while somehow maintaining itself as a whole even when there is incessant internal change. Thus the parts are in relationship with one another, the whole is greater than the sum of its parts, and the whole is able to continue and change in response to itself and to its environment.

Marriage is more than just a man plus a woman. Marriage is like a third person created between them, the "one flesh" that is greater than either one of them. The system becomes more complicated as children are added. The demand for information among members becomes even greater. Persons react differently in the family than with others. Each system operates according to its own rules, both explicit and implicit. The rules, whether functional or dysfunctional, determine the health or the disease of the system. We understand the family by understanding how members relate with one another. Persons are participants in the functions of their systems rather than mere parts. For example, if a youth makes a Teens Encounter Christ weekend and experiences a religious conversion, this will affect all members of the family. When one family member changes, the whole system either changes or resists and thus diminishes the change.

Healthy functioning family systems have several observable characteristics:

1. *A family is a wholistic system.* That system is strongest when all members are highly committed. The relationships of members to the whole family need to be functional, i.e., complementary. Yet the family system needs to support the separateness and personal development of members. Each member is responsible for his or her own part in the system, claiming his or her own mistakes and affirming others. Family leadership roles need to be strong, which makes parental presence and responsibility important.

2. *A family perceives itself as a system.* Members have an awareness of family as an "us," a sense of pride and belonging. They find a purpose and meaning in life through a common heritage, religion and belief. Members live up to values, promises and achievements, feeling a healthy guilt when they transgress. They perceive, affirm and cherish the specialness of each member as well as the whole.

3. *A family maintains itself as a system.* The healthy family has clear and strong standards, boundaries and contracts and supports family rules, limits and agreements. Family members trust that their needs will be respected and met. Family members spend time together.

4. *The family is a self-directing system.* Family environment fosters open and honest communication. Members identify problems and explore them together, seeking creative and different solutions. Members have the capacity to

adapt and change and deal openly with conflict and stressful situations.

Families need to see how they interact and communicate. Help one member of the family and everyone gets better. To insure a healthy family, we treat not only the ailing member but the whole family. We see this in treatment for a disease like alcoholism, where we bring not only the alcoholic to treatment but require the whole family to be active participants in the healing process. Family members literally give and take life from each other, not only in the natural order, but in the spiritual life as well. It is through these relationships that life and faith are passed in a healthy or unhealthy way.

Family Strengths

We have focused more on the weaknesses and hurts of families than on the strengths. To create a family spirituality, we best learn from families who manifest strong and healthy relationships. Church leaders have often defined the "good family" by faithful attendance at church services, church support, and exterior images. Spirituality invites us to look at what goes on inside the family, such as whether or not they have good communication, emotional support and trusting relationships.

The functions of the family are relational. People marry so they can love and be loved. They search for intimacy, not protection. They have children so they can give and be given to, care and be cared about, and share the joys of connecting with their posterity. If relational needs are not met in the family, people will search elsewhere for them. God's presence becomes more intense when they love each other more deeply and continues as they develop a loving community. Private Christianity is an empty reality. We find God in our relationships with each other. To be spiritual does not involve an escape from others but consists in a deeper entry into other's lives.

Dolores Curran and others have studied the characteristics of healthy families.* I contend that any search for a healthy spirituality for families will be modeled on the characteristics of healthy family living. Our efforts to help families develop a spiritual life will concentrate on developing these traits.

Family members frequently exchange compliments and express appreciation for one another. Affirming one another is the cohesive factor in all happy families. Family members like each other, and keep on acting as allies rather than competitors. The family environment is characterized by caring, trust, warmth, openness, empathy, and humor. Members feel they matter, are loved, are recognized, and are cared about. Members in healthy families are affirmed for who they are and not for what they look like, have, or do. Members support one another, for better or for worse, in similarity and in differences. They seem to find the right level of support for each member, truly knowing the capabilities, confidence, and needs of each.

When parents' praise is genuine and accurate, children learn self-love rather than conceit. Traditional spirituality thought praise spoiled people and made them vain. This spirituality stressed humility (actually, a false humility) and modesty. Praise works wonders in the family and reinforces relationships. Praise helps us all know that we are worthwhile and believe that "God does not make junk!"

Family members spend a significant amount of time together, and make an effort to insure that this happens. Healthy families are busy families, yet they are committed to one another's welfare. They take time to do enjoyable things together. The healthy family spends more time together than in activities that separate members. They give higher priority to such traits as the development of play and humor, family interaction, and shared leisure time than to a strong work ethic, financial security, and activities in the civic community. Unlike many, they do not feel guilty when they take time for play and leisure. Husbands and wives value opportunities to spend time together, paying attention to their relationship exclusive of the children. Family members balance the time spent with each individual so they can know and love each

---

*   Dolores Curran, *Traits of a Healthy Family* (New York: Balantine Books, 1983).

other. Parents make time for graduations and appendectomies. The family meal becomes the gathering place, the one time each day when parents and children are assured of uninterrupted time with each other.

The healthy family shares leisure time. Too many individuals regard nonworking time as their private possession, not to be infringed on by other members of the family. The healthy family keeps its collective leisure time in balance. The quantity of time spent with the family is important, but so is the quality. Healthy families tend to get away together, whether to visit grandparents overnight or to take an annual vacation. Children tell parents in many ways that they would rather have them than absentee parents and material possessions. Too many families use busy-ness to avoid having real relationships with one another, but healthy families find ways to come together.

Family members communicate and listen easily and well. They have the ability to share feelings, express differences of opinion, identify problems and decide on solutions. Members spend a good deal of time talking together about feelings, dreams, joys, sorrows, and hopes. They all listen well, share their own needs and wants clearly, and express feelings openly. They waste little energy on blaming and fault finding. The family is not conflict free, but faces conflicts openly, seeking to learn each others' needs and interests and to resolve difficulties in respectful "no-lose" negotiation.

Communication means risking ourselves to let another know who we really are underneath all the layers of society's shoulds and oughts. It is basic to loving relationships. Communication fuels the caring, giving, sharing, and affirming. Without genuine listening and sharing of ourselves, we can't know one another. Good communication creates the energy needed to run the family system. The more complex the system becomes, e.g., by adding members or through the normal maturation of members, the more good communication is demanded for effective living and healthy change. Without communication, families become households of roommates who react rather than respond to one another's needs.

Family members are open to change, flexible in rules and roles. When the parent(s) take strong leadership, the views of all members are invited, encouraged, heard, respected, and considered. The family respects individual differences, prizes individuality, and makes room for a wide variety of personalities, interests and differences. The family has stability and continuity in daily life, but remains adaptable enough to modify habits and routines in the face of crisis or other needs. Family members learn to live with one another, respect individuals while not necessarily approving of their behavior, and encourage individuals to make decisions appropriate to their age and to live with the consequences. The family is relatively democratic in decision-making and planning.

Family members have a sense of commitment and faithfulness to one another. The family is committed to supporting one another amd promoting each other's well-being and happiness. Members emphasize creativity and originality rather than mere conformity. They promote high levels of responsible autonomy. Surprise is still a part of joy in these relationships. Members also share responsibility. Families with good relationships tend to expect more from their children and are more willing to help others accept responsibility. Members are sensitive to the feelings of others and foster an atmosphere where all are responsible for a harmonious household.

Family members have a high degree of unity centered around a core of shared values and goals. This core of shared values and goals contributes to a sense of purpose and direction. Parents in healthy families are not afraid to talk values, continually letting the children know what they believe in. The healthier a family, the more developed is their sense of right and wrong. A sense of family is one of the most foundational traits of a healthy family. The family treasures its traditions and rituals. Traditions give the family a sense of identity, of belonging, and help make the family conscious of its uniqueness, its personality, its character, and its heritage. Their special relationship makes them a unity which has a personality.

Ritualizing is very important in families. Rituals give participants a chance to express their love and to express what is important in their life together. The healthy family has a shared religious core that provides a base of common values and a sense of purpose. Religion is a major source of strength for the family as well as for individuals. At the experiential level, children experience faith from those around them. Faith in God plays a strong role in daily family life.

Healthy families continue to experience forgiveness. Family members take responsibility for their actions, and claim their mistakes. Reconciliation is a basic part of communication. Healthy families fight, but they find time to discuss the issue heatedly, rationally, and completely, with enough time to reconcile. Reconciliation is as much the responsibility of the person who was hurt as the one who did the hurting, with the goal to restore unity.

The family has connections with other families and with the community. The family is not isolated. Members get involved in the community. The family has ties with other families with whom they socialize and who can aid and support them in times of need or crisis. Families are able to cope in a crisis because they are involved and connected with other families.

Healthy families don't happen because members concentrate first on the quality of their relationships but rather because they are involved as a family in something bigger. They extend themselves to others by offering hospitality, sharing their homes and themselves with others. They offer themselves, their tables, and their homes freely and warmly without making others feel indebted. Healthy families are generally aware of others' needs and welfare and they value service. Children grow up to be altruistic and empathetic, caring and responsible persons because of their family experiences.

Healthy families probably have as many problems as less healthy families, but they are able to admit them and seek to solve them early. Healthy families negotiate well. If the problem involves the whole family, everyone gets a chance to speak. Healthy families find support from friends and from groups of families who gather around similar problems.

Holiness is wholeness. Obviously, healthy family systems create loving family relationships, on which family spirituality builds. Unhealthy families, in contrast, tend to be at odds in their relationships, filled with shame or embarrassment about the family, find life meaningless, fear abandonment, ignore problems, and get torn apart by conflict. Family spirituality finds and celebrates the holiness and joy in family life.

Rethinking Conjugal Spirituality

An old axiom says: "You can tell a person by the walls of their home." Many hallways identify the family story by dozens of faces peering from photographs hung on the walls. Pictures of the bride and groom, a first communion, the entire family in its Sunday best, a graduate, grandparents, and special uncles and aunts speak a family history. For anyone in the family to understand who he or she is, these shared memories and the identity which binds the family together must be passed on. Frequently these pictures also proclaim the larger Christian story of which the family is a part.

The spirituality of the family spans generations and encompasses all these faces. An intertwining of destiny, of shared gifts, of collectively suffered pain makes the family a profoundly interdependent entity. The stories of the hallway gallery serve as reminders of the family traditions. Members learn who they are as family as their story is passed on and recounted within the family. The individual's history becomes richer and more meaningful within the context of the Christian story of which the family is a part.

The home holds within its walls a store of memories which offer a wealth of insight. Here members find meaning, coming to understand themselves and the world around them. Through eyes of faith they look beyond these pictures and the ordinary family they portray to see the face of God.

Families come to know that God's own life can somehow be touched here and now, in the faces, places, and events of their ordinary daily life. They live in the tension of a God with them but not fully. Something is required of them, some seeking, some response, some radical change that enables them to become more the way God wants them to be. Families have some sense that their family life is sacred, but seldom hear this affirmed. What family members know to be sacred in their marriage, lovemaking, sexual intimacy, procreation, parenting, building and repairing intimate relationships, and caring for other members is authentic and must be part of the knowledge of this gathered church.

The family's ways of being church have to do with inhabiting, co-penetration of bodies and hearts, human attachments, busyness and labors of providing, touching and being touched. Much of spirituality is rooted in human bodies. The church too often distinquished between body and spirit, seeing sexuality as an obstacle to spirituality, while marital experience says we cannot separate the two. We awaken to the physical sensations of pregnancy, to carrying, washing, feeding and caressing bodies. It is not enough to advise couples to read their Bibles, meditate, worship, pray, and do what monks and hermits did.

The new dimension of experience and knowledge brought about in a long-term physical relationship and the interpenetration of being which results make of the couple a spiritual reality fundamentally different from the individual and communal units familiar to the history of spirituality. In marriage, the self is in some sense another in addition to being itself.

A spirituality for married couples requires a radical shift from celibate spirituality. God calls most people to on-going human relationships, where agreement to share each other's lives forms the most important contract of society. They are no longer two individuals, nor are the dynamics of this relationship like that of a community. The couple is unique in their love, called forth by belief that their particular union will in some sense restore God's plan for union of man and woman as one flesh. For each couple, the end product is also unique, as they have a bond considered even closer than that of blood relationship. Yet the very present possibility of divorce has transformed marriage into a great adventure where two different individuals try to achieve a unity as they bring into reality this more-than-blood relationship by sheer act of will. The couple relationship becomes a fragile miracle dependent on the continued willingness of the partners to be in relationship. Conjugal spirituality has to do with the mystery of forming this relationship, the discipline of its continuance, and the rewards of its achievement.

Most couples have moments when they sense they are in the presence of a mystery greater than themselves, e.g., learning of a first pregnancy, shared vulnerability during intercourse, reconciliation after misunderstanding, or the birth of a child. These unique moments reveal the mysterious reality that lies at the heart of a marital relationship, a twofold dynamic of intimacy and otherness which form the spirituality of marriage.

Desire to be in union with a chosen person of the opposite sex is simultaneously a desire to be in union with the life of God in oneself. To become united with a man or a woman or with God, a person must cultivate an expansive capacity for intimacy. Intimacy means being vulnerable and transparent enough to allow a spouse to touch one's deepest being and to be changed by the relationship as spouses know and are known in a unique way. Oriented toward individualism, Americans do not easily open themselves to this painful transformation demanded by the intimate encounter of married life.

When a man and woman become one, they remain at the same time two. A quality of otherness about this union remains as much a part of the spirality of marriage as is the quality of intimacy. They face the unalterable dignity of each person and the equal dignity of marriage partners. One person does not own the other, nor is one subject to the whim or will of the other. They are to be responsive to one another, but not dominated or dominating. Each is utterly free to choose to love the other. The sense of otherness comes also from the recognition that each has unique interests, backgrounds and goals which can change persons and teach something of God's ways.

The tension of living between the two dynamics of intimacy and otherness constitutes the spiritual art of marriage. Mutuality calls them to recognize each other's full dignity in this partnership while freely entering into the covenanted union of intimacy. Mutual discernment, the delicate process of lovingly listening to one's self, the other, and to God, forms the center of Christian marriage.

Self-reflection, both individual and communal, is utterly necessary for any continuing growth into the image and likeness of God. Couples are caught in the tension between getting rid of the materialism that invades our lives and stands in the way of God and the impulse to provide, shelter, feed, clothe, care for, teach, and provide stability for their family. The virtue of fidelity calls spouses to reserve the most intimate expressions of love for each other alone while constantly juggling priorities to be attentive to the good of each individual in the family as well as the whole family and extended family members.

Prolonged harmony between two human beings is without doubt the hardest thing one can ever attempt. A couple's growth is based on communicating and relating. They must master the powerful force of sex. Talk and sex are natural, but using them to create lasting intimacy is neither natural nor simple. Talk and sex are religious exercises that form a couple's spirituality. Of all the tools of conjugal spirituality, strong emphasis should be placed on sexual intercourse, the ongoing physical dialogue unique to the couple which transforms them in a God-like temporary fusing of bodies and souls.

Parental Spirituality

A couple's love for each other, which God uses to enflesh new human life, leads to a parental spirituality which is quite incarnational. God's creative power is present in the human loving acts of husband and wife. Through their love, the unconditional love of 'GOD WITH US' gains new earthly expression.

Catholics have identified women's role with the home more than that of men. It may be easier to see woman's spirituality connected to the home because of her natural functions in parenting, but the spirituality of both men and women is framed by the home setting. We cannot separate body and soul for either women or men. Women may give more attention to the experiences of being entered, the cyclical wetness and dryness of fertility and infertility, the menstrual cycle, the body changes of pregnancy and nursing a baby, and to the care of infant's bodies. Yet men share in these rhythms and celebrations of life.

Pregnancy means a time of waiting similar to believers' waiting for God. Spouses share the mystery that God has chosen them for the gift of life and the ground out of which the incarnate God flowers in our world. Pregnancy means listening to the budding new life. Creation of another person calls upon a woman's body to use all of its available resources. For both husband and wife, there is attentiveness to the presence of another, a sensitivity to the new life cohabiting the deep recesses of the mother's body.

Pregnancy is a contemplative time, waiting as a new life unfolds in union with God as co-creator. Aware they are now different, couples embrace a new intimacy because this surprising presence lives in the mother. They wait for the blossoming physical changes that signal the new life which becomes the center of their focus.

Parents incarnate God's presence, which comes through the longing of their hearts and the labors of their bodies. Pregnancy reminds them they do not give life without suffering and giving of the very substance of who they are. In that pain, a reminder of the paschal mystery, parents begin to understand communion, compassion, and participatory love.

Pregnancy lies at the heart of the Christian message. A pregnant woman is bound, at the most intimate center of her being, to another being, linked by the tissues of her body to another life and through that life to all other lives. Waiting for God's life to grow and enter the world through them, parents become aware of a greater life of which they are a part, the creative and redemptive process of our God. Parents are the place of advent, the womb through which the living God is born.

Any parent knows what it means to welcome a child. It radically changes one's life. Parents accept responsibility for another person twenty-four hours a day, seven days a week, for a good many years and, ultimately, they welcome the unfolding mystery of an entire lifetime of joys and pains as their own. To welcome a child is to give priority to the unpredictability of another life, to allow plans and dreams to be altered because of another's need, to see one's own capacity to love expand and to confront the shattering truth of personal self-centeredness.

To welcome a child or any family member asks one to open their heart a little more. The heart acquires a capacity to love a little differently, to respond with compassion to a new personality, to willingly participate in the drama of unfolding life. It also involves allowing the love for those with whom one is intimate – spouse, parent, child, friend – to become transparent enough that the love of God can be seen through it. Parents learn more about the source of love, God, through the experiences of parenting.

Mothers continue their discovery through the nursing relationship. Nursing means much more than giving nourishment. The spiritual dimension comes alive with attentiveness and sensitivity to the needs of someone else. Mothers learn to take care of themselves so that they might meet the needs of another, nourishing their own bodies, getting sufficient rest, and structuring activities to be available.

Mothers also learn what it means to give of their own substance. Nursing draws upon one's deepest, most essential body resources. A mother must be there, she must be food, she must allow herself to be given over to another person. She learns the meaning of the communion meal through the art of giving her own life energy in the nursing bond. She is called to be food and drink for another person, to give life, and to realize something of the fullness of life that Jesus holds out to us.

Holding a child is also a spiritual experience. As children grow older and need to identify themselves apart from their parents, they often do not want to be held. Many parents feel sadness and desolation when a child comes back pregnant, broken by drugs, or alone and afraid, needing to be held. They open their arms to embrace their child as did the prodigal's father.

The prodigal child returning home has come to the end of all resources. She or he comes home not only to find the welcome and nurture of a parent's embrace but to find that human needfulness is indeed blessed. The prodigal discovers the richness of being poor in spirit, the comfort in mourning, the strength in mercy. Nestled in the parent's arms, he or she finds that expansive love which nurtures all brothers and sisters with loving care.

Sensing their limitations and startled by the experience of vulnerability, parents let go of their illusion of self-sufficiency and reach out to greater sources of strength and grace. They also need loving arms. Persons called to be providers, shelterers, healers, and teachers for their children easily forget their own neediness. They need reminders they too are children whose hearts must be open, trusting, and in need of God's deep embrace. To move deeply into the circle of God's arms involves a radical entry into one's own vulnerability and need.

The deep attachment to a child is nurtured and grows over many years. When parents' hearts have become stretched to make a special place for that unique love, they do not shrink again when the loved one leaves the nest or dies. Letting go does not consist in ceasing to love or detaching oneself, but in loving more. Letting go involves radical faith. It means entrusting what one most loves to the expansive care and protection of God. Hearts are stretched and torn to love beyond self. To let go is to love like and allow oneself to be loved by God.

Family Spirituality

Most lives are crammed with work, school, hobbies, meetings, sports, social activities, and helping others. Family life needs precious time for leisure and wonder. Too often frantic activities separate people from each other. Families need precious or sacred time to play together, sit silently watching a sunset, walk through the fall leaves, or sit and enjoy the ocean. When persons find time to enjoy a cup of coffee together, to sit on the edge of the bed and talk about the concerns of the day, or to be genuinely present to each other, they experience time for wonder and time to watch for God.

The family needs time for ritual and celebration. A simple ritual like burning one's baptismal candle on a baptismal feast day or sharing memories while looking at the family photo album make these special times of watching for God. Birthdays are sacred times, where the individual's story becomes part of the larger story of the family and people of the God who brings us all to birth. Vacations and days off offer sacred times for families, with a walk in the mountains, a picnic by a stream, a day to do family chores together, a Sunday meal with grandparents, or family reunions. Families' sacred days and seasons are times of discovery and surprise, times of lingering and listening and seeing with new eyes.

An old axiom says: "The odor of sanctity in the home is the smell of freshly-baked bread." The family gathers in common at table to enact the ritual of being a community of mutual need and nourishment. To prepare and share a meal together is one of the holiest acts in religious tradition. To eat together is a communion with one another.

There is a reality to "us" as a family that transcends the individuals in it. Fully realized, the family's togetherness has a special life and quality all its own that approaches the divine in whose image they are made. They live fully when they live with and for each other, recognizing that their individuality contributes to and is enhanced by the rest of the community.

To be in communion with one another means to share lives at the deepest levels. Members are mutually dependent upon each other, so one's gifts and another's needs fit together. To be in communion also means that when people open themselves to become aware of their shared life and to live accordingly, they genuinely begin to be one body. That body is greater than the sum of its parts, the body of Christ. God's presence can only be there when they allow themselves to acknowledge their mutual need and nourishment, when they bring the fullness of who they are to be gift for each other and to be recipients of each other's gifts. They come as well to humbly acknowledge their shortcomings and abuses as a family, and to ask forgiveness from God and one another.

Forgiveness is the mystery at the heart of the spiritual vitality of family life. Persons have the capacity to reclaim love by forgiving one another. God's creative capacity for healing the human community lies in the mystery of forgiveness, where people have a powerful recreative gift by which they can free themselves and others from terrible bondage. Real growth in intimacy occurs in reconciliation after a falling out.

Families are communities called to offer and accept forgiveness together. Opportunities exist daily because family members live in such proximity. Being together sets up numerous occasions for family members to admit that they have hurt and failed one another, to ask forgiveness, and to freely offer to forgive. Sometimes that forgiveness must be offered in the midst of searing misery or the anquish of betrayal.

Hospitality is one of the strongest demands of the Bible. In welcoming a visitor, we welcome the Christ. Hospitality means not only that the person is fed and cared for, but is likewise refreshed by the experience of being appreciated and valued for the God-given uniqueness of his or her person. Families extend the gift of hospitality in many ways. They welcome others and share the love generated within the family. Hospitality engenders a sense of celebration and play when families plan a surprise birthday party for an unsuspecting friend, gather with others for an evening of prayer, offer room to out-of-town visitors, or gather friends to celebrate an anniversary with ice cream. The family that makes space and takes time for others is enriched immeasurably in return.

As persons reflect on the mystery of life, they experience the need to give thanks. All they have is given. Life itself is a gift. They are the recipients of time, of the gracious earth, of each other's lives. Acquiring the spirit of gratitude serves to heighten their awareness of God's gifts.

While we have looked at spirituality here as reflected in the lives of healthy intact families, we must also affirm the spirituality found in single-parent families, families in pain, and individuals who at best are members of extended families. God lives and moves intimately within the fabric of human life even in the most desperate and painful events. In the experience of absence, we encounter a different face of our God.

In their longing for one another when they are apart, families often experience God as absence. Children, e.g., may be deprived of a family by prolonged illness or the divorce of parents. In this longing itself, a sign of the deep bond of love that connects them, the family can recognize the vibrant touch of God. Love, when severed, shattered, or constrained, shows itself as the dark face of absence. The habitual tension between an exacting parent and an unwilling teenager, the desperate loneliness of a couple whose intimate life has turned cold or hostile, or the disjointed reality of a family caught in the disease of alcoholism prove experiences of the absence of

God. Yet in the very frustration, even the fearful darkness of brokenness, people can find God in the very longing to be reunited, healed, and whole. God is there in the pain of human limitations and fragility.

Families today are hungry for a new face of God not constrained by churchy identity. They are looking for a glimpse of God who they know, deeply within, is truly present to them, a God who may greet them amidst the dirty laundry, the fussing baby and the demands of job pressures as well as in their Sunday best. That God wears the faces of those whose lives we share. The parish goal is to help families find this God who breaks, bleeds, and celebrates with us.

Actions to Consider

• Family systems help us understand why we need to minister to the whole family, not to individuals. Spirituality is relationship oriented. What we do with intense love in the laundry room, the kitchen and the bedroom has to do with spirituality. Talk about how family spirituality is built on relationships. Look at parish ministries in terms of the impact on the entire family.

• Family-centered programs could focus on the list of family strengths. Perhaps a series in which various couples share how they live one of these strengths in their family. Adult education is often best accomplished by sharing of stories, which help people identify their own story and potential for what they can become.

• Ask help to connect people's faith with daily life. I have shared a good Advent series on the waiting of pregnancy. I've heard a woman talk about how she best understood Eucharist through her experience of nursing a baby. Families who have had a pregnant teenager, a teen on drugs, or a rebellious teen have some powerful stories on reconciliation within the entire family. Your listeners will identify with these sharings.

• "Forgiveness is the mystery at the heart of the spiritual vitality of family life." Every family has need for forgiveness. This is especially true in families with lots of pain. Look for opportunities to help with family reconciliation. A funeral liturgy, where a teen who killed his friend by reckless driving asked forgiveness from the parents, then from the other family members, and finally from all adults for the foolishness of youth, led to reconciliation within the two families and inspired many in the congregation to ask forgiveness from others.

• Communication is the number one problem in family relationships. Prayer is also communication, and people struggle to listen and communicate with God as readily as with members of the family. A series on communication might look at both family communication and prayer, since prayer has do both with communication with God and within the family. Many families would like to learn to pray together better.

• Encourage families to develop a family commitment statement. Such a commitment of members to a common family belief system might include such issues as acceptance of all family members, response to member's needs, time together, family worship, or a monthly family day. A commitment to the family system helps members celebrate the spirit of family and translate their convictions into daily living, i.e., to be a family-centered church.

8

Sent Two by Two

You share in one and the same mission that he gives to the whole church. You carry out that mission of the church in the home in ordinary ways.

WE HEAR THE WORD *ECOLOGY* FREQUENTLY TODAY, REFERRING to how an interacting system of organisms function together in their environment. Environmentalists make us aware how disturbing one part of the environmental ecology has a detrimental influence on the whole. We can speak as readily of an ecology of society or of the church. Some see an unhealthy church now built on a child-centered approach to religious education and a "save-your-own-soul" approach to church life. Many parents complain that the parochial school or religious education program failed to give their children faith while individualism continues the privatization of religion. One blatantly absent piece for an ecologically sound church is a sense of mission.

Mission lies at the heart of our identity as church. The church is simultaneously a community gathered in response to our life in Christ and a mission to witness to God's love by our love for the world. The mission to continue the work of Jesus and the Holy Spirit takes precedence over community. The church is always tempted to invert this priority, paying more attention to the inward community than to its primary gospel mission. Emphasis since Vatican II has focused on renewal of church institutions and structures more than on the mission of the people of God.

Most people find the locus of their Christian life in the family, the place where they are most conscious of their Christian calling and commitment. The family-centered church, like the parish church and the institutional church, is usually more committed to system maintenance than to mission. Marriage and family are not incidental but essential to our understanding of the vocation and mission of the laity. Thus, a very direct link exists between the mission of the family and the mission of the church.

Mission awareness demands a paradigm shift for the American family. Americans have already changed paradigms for the family several times. The seventeenth- and eighteenth-century family took almost sole responsibility for such needs as employment, health care, education, socialization, recreation, reproduction, identity, love and affection. This family, characterized by paternal decision-making, fixed roles, and rigid principles, achieved stability through tradition. Individual autonomy merged in service to the family unit.

In the twentieth century, family life built more commonly on a democratic, companionship model. Since the power of the father over his children was greatly diminished, children generally made their own choice of occupation and marriage partner. Women were no longer subordinate, although they had their own sphere of family responsibilities. The family now shared most responsibilities, other than identity, love and affection, with other institutions. The democratic decision-making between husband and wife was based upon interpersonal needs, with less-defined roles hinging upon personal choice and competence. This family valued equal partnership and relationships built on mutual friendship. Members experienced God, they believed, through shared communication and mutuality. Evolution of the open, democratic family, allowing greater participation by all family members, paralleled the advance of greater participation within the local church.

In the latter part of this century we moved toward a family based on individualism and personalism. With it, we watched the divorce rate and the remarriage rate soar. Single, single-again, and remarried families champion individual rights and interests. This model of family is generally characterized by few boundaries, rules and responsibilities outside the self. A primary goal is to promote self-fulfillment of family members. Individual rights and interests are highly valued. These families believe that God's call to discipleship comes primarily to the individual and must be discovered in the search for individual autonomy and authenticity.

Marriage and family, traditionally considered as defenses against individualism, now seem permeated by the "me" generation. Marriage exclusively focused on personal fulfillment and dependent on romantic love cuts spouses off from the social and kinship supports and commitments needed to sustain their relationship through times of difficulty. This creates the perilous situation in which the inner-directed and isolated nuclear family currently finds itself.

In the New Testament perspective, Jesus, who is sent by the Father, gathers a community of disciples who are to pattern their life and relationships after him. Disciples are to mirror in their lives the central gospel command to love. James reminds us that this love must be effective, not a mere sentiment. A modern axiom remnds us: "The love in your heart wasn't put there to stay. Love isn't love until you give it away." *The family has the mission of showing the church and the world what true love is.* Mission, then, is central to the identity of the family centered church and not peripheral.

Obligation Versus Individualism

Americans believe in love as the basis for enduring relationships. But they also believe in the self. The very sharing that promises to be the fulfillment of love can also threaten the self. People are afraid to lose themselves in sharing too completely with another. In *Habits of the Heart*, Robert Bellah sees Americans torn between love as an expression of spontaneous inner freedom and personal choice and love as a firmly planted, permanent commitment with obligations that transcend the immediate feelings or wishes of the partners. Bellah calls the first image of love, found among therapists, their clients, and middle-class Americans, the "therapeutic attitude," while he also recognizes the traditional view of love and marriage based on obligation and found among certain groups of Christians.

This Christian view takes seriously John's insight that only the person who knows God can know the meaning of love and Paul's sense that love is the highest and greatest gift of the Spirit. We decide to love people by action and will for their good, not because we enjoy it but because God commands this love. Obligation comes before free choice. Love means putting others' interests ahead of our own. Christians seek some of the same sharing and intimacy in marriage that other Americans seek, but they are determined to seek these within the framework of binding commitments. They believe a permanent relationship can only be achieved though an obligation to something higher than one's own fulfillment or preferences. They consciously resist the dangers of excessive individualism.

At the opposite pole, the therapeutic attitude is based on self-realization rather than with a set of external obligations. People seek autonomy, believing they can enjoy the full benefits of a love relationship only if they are independent and free to express their feelings. Thus the therapeutic model sees the individual as able to be the source of his or her own standards, to love self before asking for love from others, and to rely on his or her own judgment without deferring to others. The ideal for love, then, is not self-sacrifice but self-assertion. Persons need to be independent enough to make their own contribution to the relationship rather than doing only what the other wants. A pure therapeutic attitude denies all forms of obligation and commitment in relationships, replacing them only with the ideal of fully sharing one's feelings with a partner. The central virtue of love then becomes communication.

Most Americans waffle between the ideals of obligation and freedom. The language and some assumptions of the therapeutic attitude penetrate deeply into American culture, reinforcing individualism and encouraging people to seek their own interests and to discover the inner self. No binding obligations and no wider social understanding justify a relationship.

What has this to do with mission? How we think about love defines the meaning we give our lives in relation to the wider society. For most people, the bond to spouse and children is the most fundamental social tie. The confusion and uncertainty with which we think about love embody the difficulty we have thinking about social relationships in general.

When we focus on relationships that will meet our needs rather than on commitment to others, any sense of mission is quite removed.

Family ministry best thrives with a sense of commitment and permanence. Christian spouses find their relationships deepened by being part of a wider set of purposes and meanings. Most married Americans have difficulty articulating reasons for their commitment beyond the self. While they want enduring relationships, they resist the notion that this may involve obligations and sacrifices beyond the wishes of the partners. They are uncomfortable with the Christian's idea of sacrifice as an expression of Christian love. Since the only measure of the good is what is good for the self, something that burdens the self cannot be a part of love. Americans find it difficult to overcome the sharp distinction between self and other.

The family is no longer an integral part of a larger moral ecology tying the individual to the community, church, and nation. We make family the core of the private sphere, where we aim not to link individuals to the public sphere but to avoid ties as far as possible. Consumerism and television augment this tendency. Americans are seldom as selfish as the therapeutic culture urges them to be, but the family circle often defines the limit of their altruism. Taking care of one's own becomes more imbedded when joined with suspicion and withdrawl from the world.

We face a major challenge to integrate what we take for granted about personal relations in marriage with a sense of broader obligations. Marriage commits us to a whole framework of life, which sustains the love of the partners, but which also must be explained in terms of family, community, church, and wider society. Catholic teaching needs to find a way to affirm the dignity, freedom, and happiness of persons in marriage and family while simultaneously linking parenthood, kinship, and social roles to the integrity of sex and marriage as embodied and social experiences.

A personalist paradigm is incomplete even though it raises a new awareness of relationship in marriage. A more adequate paradigm would embrace a sense of the family called by God as a unit to continue the mission of Jesus.

When Avery Dulles looked for a model for the church, he ultimately settled on a community of disciples model, which suggests a paradigmatic model for the family. "Marriage," Dulles says, "is a sacrament of discipleship. It is the commitment of a man and a woman to the joint venture of discipleship together, in which each helps the other advance in the following of Jesus."[*]

In discussing spirituality, we talked about family systems. The family system is our strength; yet we have not learned how to make family life our number one priority. Our society fails us by isolating each of us from our primary family systems. At the very time we need each other most, we find ourselves detached, isolated from the most powerful source of healing and happiness.

Despite those therapists who point to the harm done by the intense intimacy of a family system gone wrong, the family is generally not a sick place and suffers more from neglect. Persons who see their lives as connected are healthier than those who spend their emotional energy breaking away to chase self-fulfillment. Families are where we learn what "us" means, especially the power of the family system to energize and cause growth even in times of suffering. In the family, every member shares responsibility for the development of every other member.

Our assumptions about family are clearly reflected in our ministerial style. In the recent past, we gave high priority to marriage preparation, family enrichment and parenting, while more recently we have emphasized spiritual ministry, personal faith development, and social outreach. We find ourselves caught in the shifting paradigms from hierarchical to partnership styles. This reflects a change from church culture to a mission community. In the pre-Vatican II church, bent on church maintenance, individuals and families derived not only fulfillment of their spiritual needs but also of many of their social, educational, and recreational needs from the parish. For most Christians today, church is a voluntary organization. Meaningful work (vocation) and intimate relationships (fam-

---

[*] Avery Dulles, *A Church to Believe In* (New York: Crossroad, 1982), pp. 13-14.

ily) form the center of life for most adults. Family ministry in the parish church must serve the vocation of work and the nurturing of relationships as the heart of its mission. Equipping families with skills to love and to live their discipleship in the home and the workplace will enable them to become the family centered church.

The Family's Mission

We often get confused between mission and ministry. Jesus' mission was to proclaim the good news of the kingdom by inviting people to intimacy with his Father. He ministered to the needs of the lame, blind, deaf and poor. Both mission and ministry are essential for the well-being of the body of Christ and its purposes within and outside the community. Mission involves creating disciples to share in the life of the Eucharistic community, and requires a personal investment and relationship with people to reveal the presence of God to them. Ministry focuses on meeting the material, psychological, physical and spiritual needs of people, providing what is lacking in their lives. Ministry does not necessarily require a deep personal investment or a deep relationship with the recipients. Others than Christians can feed the hungry, even though they are not part of the mission which flows directly from a life of intimacy with Jesus in the community of faith.

The mission of the church is clear. Jesus commanded the disciples to go into the whole world and preach the gospel to every nation (Mark 16:15). The church strives to penetrate and change the world. Missionary work is required of the larger church and, therefore, of its smaller units, including the family-centered church. For the family to be a miniature church, it must do what the church does. The family is called to be a hope, a sign, a sacrament that shows forth the love of God in the world. The place of the church in the twenty-first century depends on the family. The family has such a vital role in transforming the world that we can truly say with John Paul II that "the path to the future passes through the family" (FC, 85).

When we speak of the mission of the family, we are speaking of something unique. No individual person or group can carry on the work of mission in the same way as the family does. The family is uniquely equipped for mission and serves as a model for all mission efforts in the bigger church. The sacrament of matrimony is essential to this understanding of mission. The heart of the family is a sacramental couple who see their marriage as a vocation for the sake of the church. This does not imply that other forms of family, such as single parent families, lack a sense of mission.

Married life is essentially connected to the life of the Christian community. Couples receive support from and give enrichment to the wider covenantal community. Growth in intimacy cannot happen in a marriage fostering individualism. The ethical and spiritual impact of changing marriage to a contractual agreement which lacks the mutual giving and receiving of persons sharing life is tremendous.

Joseph Epstein writes: "What the loss of a sense of community involves – and involves not abstractly but quite concretely – is the loss of the ability to imagine that one's actions have any consequence outside one's own life. Once this has taken place, certain priorities follow, among them the accompanying loss of the ability to imagine anything more important that one's own happiness."* Hope for overcoming this deadly selfishness lies with the church which, if faithful to its call as the body of Christ, implicitly values community. This community properly witnesses its support not only at the wedding liturgy but throughout the marriage by ongoing service to a couple living the church's sacrament of marriage.

Married couples bear responsibility to enhance the intimacy of other couples. Members of the community challenge each other with their love and support. Faith communities need to get more involved in the issues, concerns, and values of married life. If the community does not get involved, they leave couples subject to the influences of a society destructive of marriage.

The basis of family mission begins with the couple themselves. They are called to a life of intimacy and belonging to one another modeled on Christ's relationship to the church.

---

* Joseph Epstein, *Divorced in America* (New York: E.P. Dutton, 1974) p. 95.

Their goal is not peaceful coexistence but unity, not merely for their own joy but for the sake of the church. God created humans for a love which identifies us and gives us purpose.

Baptized into the body of Christ, Christians are drawn into the mission of Jesus, commissioned (co-missioned) to extend God's love: "As you have sent me into the world, I have sent them into the world" (John 17:18). This baptismal mission takes special form in matrimony. Spouses devotion to one another and the resultant lifestyle of tenderness and complete belonging form the underpinnings of their mission in the church. Sexual intimacy will set the tone for their total way of life together and affect the quality of their mission as family. The totality of their immersion in one another is the greatest gift the couple can bring to the church.

Teilhard de Chardin said: "Sexual passion serves Christ. It is a redeeming act as well as a creative one." When a couple greatly desire each other, they make present in their lives and to the church the God who is love. Therefore, the sexual dimension of a couple's love is not a private affair for them alone, but serves the welfare of the church. It provides an atmosphere of creative and redemptive love in the body of Christ.

The children born into a sacramental marriage are also integral to the mission of the family, because they are an incarnation of the couple's love. Family mission is more than meeting each other's needs. It requires the members of the family to be living in relationship with one another. The very quality of the family relationship is vital to their mission.

One basic principle is that the family view its mission and service as something the whole family be involved in together. It becomes self-defeating if serving others becomes another way of fragmenting the family. This easily happens, for example, if parents become so involved in helping others that they neglect their children, who may end up resenting the church. When a family regularly serves together, both parents and children feel a positive impact. Involvement alongside the parents is one of the best forms of religious education a child can receive, part of the church's teaching mission. Children learn from experience that faith is a way of life and that a

Christian commitment makes a real difference in the way a person chooses to live.

Living the meaning of family not just as a model but as a leaven, Christian families call the people of the church to live as the family of God. By their extraordinary willingness to forgive and be reconciled with one another, they call the whole church to recognize its call to be a forgiving people. Aware that they have been chosen for each other as a sacrament or sign of God's loving presence, they see themselves as more than just ordinary persons living marriage. Their sense of worth comes from the one who chose them, not from themselves. They are not better than others, but different because they have been chosen by God.

God chose a people to be the church, not simply individuals who belong to God in isolation from one another. We are to be immersed in each other's lives, thus experiencing loving and being loved which allows us to make the radical choice to be intimate with others and thus find meaning, identity, and joy in life. Our communion with God involves communion with one another. The church is, then, to be a community of intimates, and married couples produce this church. The mission of married people is to incarnate God's love in a symbol that is credible and attractive. The witness of the sexual love of a couple thus extends far beyond each family circle. Couples who witness this love in their sexual response must take part in the church's altruistic concern for the well-being of all people.

The fruitfulness of marriage is thus rooted in the very nature of love. Spouses must love others also, lest they become locked in a jealous exclusiveness that defeats both the symbolism and the efficacious power of their sacramental love. Their love must be fruitful, extending obviously to their children, but also to finding a brother or sister in the starving children and victims of war viewed on international television or among those in need in the neighborhood.

Spouses have to be concerned about future generations, too, which implies conservation of the earth's resources. If they don't care about ending world hunger and racism, they deny the intrinsic symbolism and meaning of sexual intercourse. Individualism, of course, denies that the motive for sexual love extends beyond a spouse to future generations. In reality, a close and direct connection exists between global concern for justice and peace and sexual intimacy in marriage.

The primary mission of the family is to reveal the church to itself. It will take much more than words to transform our parishes into a communion of people. The mission of the family is doomed to frustration and failure so long as the environment in the church blocks the family from being a force for renewal. Liberation of the family begins by recognizing the rightful place of the sacrament of matrimony in the treasure of the church. Sacramental couples are living signs of God's urgent call to live as church in a relationship of unconditional love with one another.

The gospel is incompatible with the today's message of self-fulfillment. When church leaders champion the values of independence and personalism above those of belonging and self-giving, the values vital to family will be rejected or ignored. Unfortunately, the clergy, religious, and professional laity who control the vision and decisions in the church today, too easily forget the meaning of the gospel they first learned and shared in their childhood homes. No place now exists for the married as couples at this level of church life, e.g., including sacramental couples in the decision-making process.

Married couples can witness and speak to values of relationship in all areas of church life and renewal. They help us hear the gospel's call to relationship, to intimacy, to communion with one another in Christ, rather than to self-fulfillment apart from community. They offer outsiders not only the faith but the faithful. When they live the command to love, spousal love reaches beyond personal preference and attraction to exclude no one.

Beyond the Family

For some years, church leaders and politicians have proclaimed the need to stabilize family life. John Paul II terms the family "the first and fundamental structure for 'human ecology'" because this is where personhood and the experience of love begin. In *Familiaris Consortio*, he challenged families to "become what you are." When families recognize their interdependence with each other and with God, this becoming will be enhanced. As sharer in the mission of the church, the family has a role to play in the renewal of society.

How does the family foster this response to the larger world? Some ways include stewardship, acceptance, and outreach. Stewardship involves our attitude toward, and treatment of, all our resources. One of the most precious resources available to us is the earth itself. Families can make an enormous contribution to the ailing health of our planet by showing genuine concern for the earth, the habitat to all living things including themselves. The way families treat their material resources ties in closely with concern for the earth and its inhabitants. Families of faith will want to resist the temptation to unbridled consumerism, which tips the balance of economic distribution toward the affluent and away from the poor. Recycling provides a good way to learn care for the resources of the earth, and an alms box offers a good way to learn the practice of sharing with others. Family spirituality cannot be separated from a simple lifestyle.

The whole of Jesus' mission is a direct challenge to his followers to live more simply and to be more responsible and accountable for what they have. It is hard to be serious stewards of the earth without seeing the tremendous responsibility this entails for protecting human life. This concern for life can also direct us to work toward changing social and economic conditions that threaten life. A simpler lifestyle can free our time and attention for enriching our relationships with others. The needs of others deserve precedence over looking at everything in terms of one's own use. Families might practice stewardship by opening their home to others in ways such as foster care, inviting lonely people to share a meal, or acts of service rather than self-interest.

In a society still riddled with prejudice, ignorance and fear of persons perceived as different from ourselves, acceptance of differences within the family can be a natural step towards acceptance of those beyond the family parameters. Every dimension of home life reflects certain values. The books and magazines we read, TV programs we watch, friends we invite to our homes, schools we attend, and churches we join have a powerful formative impact on children's attitudes toward those perceived as different from themselves.

How can families create an environment that encourages a sense of respect for people from a variety of races and cultures in a society that works to keep groups of people apart from each other and fosters the growth of false ideas and fears? Prejudice, discrimination, and the oppressive dynamic of racism have torn at the foundation of the Kingdom for centuries. Families can work individually and corporately in society to make Jesus' vision "that all may be one" a reality. They might take their lead from the U. S. Catholic Bishops: "We should influence the members of our families, especially our children, to be sensitive to the authentic human values and cultural contributions of each racial grouping in our country. . . . The difficulties of these new times demand a new vision and a renewed courage to transform our society and achieve justice for all."*

Stewardship and acceptance can be expressed largely within the home environment. Outreach, however, moves families directly into the community at large. Through outreach the family participates more visibly in the social witness and mission of the church. Many Christian families see the larger society as a threat to their cherished family values. A problem arises when families believe they can only realize values such as intimacy, trust and fidelity by moving away from society into the protection of their home. The family cannot realize its full potential as family by itself but only in relation to society as a whole.

Dolores Leckey reminds us that "Outreach is as essential to the identity of the Christian family as prayer and worship." James and Kathleen McGinnis add: "Family values are realized not only by 'spending more time with the family' but also by participating as a family and with other families in the transformation of the world. . . . Family community is built in part on participation in the building of neighborhood and global community."**

---

* *Brothers and Sisters to Us: U.S. Bishops' Pastoral Letter on Racism in Our Day.*
** Recurrent theme of James and Kathleen McGuiness, *Parenting for Peace and Justice* (Maryknoll, N.Y.: Orbis Books, 1990).

Families need the community to overcome the natural resistance to engaging in social concerns. This resistance comes from many sources: fear of involvement, time and energy constraints, discouragement at the overwhelming nature of many social problems, and feelings of being ill-equipped and poorly informed. Individual families benefit from the encouragement, equipping, and inspiration that come from the larger church and from other committed families.

Families are being victimized by the social forces in our materialistic society, where objects are becoming more important than persons, while persons are often treated as objects. A dramatic rise in child abuse and spouse abuse reflects the violence of our society. Families need not remain passive victims in the face of these social forces. When we help families to see themselves as church, we open wonderful possibilities for empowering them to be agents of change. With this understanding, we see church not as a safe harbor to protect us from the world but as a leaven in society, deeply involved in transforming the world.

The family-centered church is the primary place where individuals are affirmed and develop their gifts. Affirmation is essential to the church's social mission, as persons cannot be concerned about others unless they first feel good about themselves. In the *Challenge of Peace,* the U.S. Bishops asked parents to "consciously discuss issues of justice." Children who work through some painful experiences and discuss issues of injustice in their own lives as well as in the larger world come to see that adults are concerned and doing something about those social evils.

Prayer and worship hold special importance in the family-centered church. Family reconciliation services can help remove barriers and build community. Prayer centered around family decision-making internalizes values and creates responsibility. The more a family feels unity, the more willing it generally is to go out into the world as a family. And the more the family as a whole involves itself in community and the larger world, the more it usually comes together.

Just as the parish church or community should experience a sense of being sent forth into the world from its celebration of the Eucharist, so too the family as domestic church needs to feel sent forth. Parish community and family community are called to extend the love members experience in these communities to the world outside. Each is called to be a leaven in the transformation of the world.

Family as Evangelizer

John Paul II assigns the highest priority in the mission of the church to evangelization. Yet most Catholics feel little responsibility for spreading the faith. Evangelization, according to Vatican II, is a duty of every Christian.* All the laity are expected to cooperate in the work of evangelization, especially in the environment of their work and family life (LG, 35).

Paul VI stated that evangelization is in fact the grace and vocation proper to the church, her deepest identity. The church exists to evangelize. In Evangelization in the Modern World, he added: "It is unthinkable that a person accept the Word of God and give himself to the kingdom without, in truth, becoming a person who proclaims and bears witness to it" (Para 71).

At Puebla, John Paul II emphasized that the church tends through evangelization to "contribute to the construction of a new society that is more fraternal and just" (Puebla, 12). In *Christifideles Laici*, he stated that the family, as "domestic church," can be a powerful instrument of evangelization. On his tour of the United States in 1987, John Paul II added: "The family is the first setting of evangelization, the place where the Good News of Christ is first received, and then, in simple yet profound ways, handed on from generation to generation." Since the family is the primary cell of the Christian community, it follows that families should evangelize families. The ideals and values upon which the family is founded are precisely the ideals and values for which many people long. The Christian family proclaims that the meaning of life is to be found in a human intimacy which is experienced as inseparable from intimacy with God.

Evangelization is an integral part of Christian living. Because we all long for a loving God who can satisfy our inborn

---

*   *Lumen Gentium*, 16-17.

craving, the ordinary Christian family can be a powerful agent in proclaiming the gospel. Its life together gives witness to the fulfillment to be found by those who base their lives on human intimacy and intimacy with God.

None of the church's efforts to set up evangelization programs will match the importance and effectiveness of ordinary Christian families when they do their best to live the Christian life. Actions, especially the way we treat others, speak louder than words. By the witness of its daily life, the family allows the spirit of Christ to shine forth. Paul VI said: "Through this wordless witness these Christians stir up irresistible questions in the hearts of those who see how they live. . . . Such a witness is already a silent proclamation of the Good News and a very powerful and effective one."

By serving one another and by their dedication to serving the needs of others, the family evangelizes. Catholics are hesitant to proclaim their faith with confidence, aware that American tradition makes religion a purely private matter. As John Paul II asserts, "Faith is strengthened when it is given to others."[*]

This does not mean pushing our faith on others. The family-centered church evangelizes itself first, so that faith shapes their whole life. Self-evangelization reinforces in our own mind and heart an identity we have adopted, one which makes us different from many others. The Christian family views life and the world in ways that differ, sometimes considerably, from the perspectives of a secular culture.

Parents find themselves with a special role to play in the evangelization that goes on within the family. They remain at all times during their children's growing-up years their most influential and effective catechists. Parental actions remain more important than words, but actions without verbal commentary may not have as great an impact on the child as will a combination of the two.

Evanglization goes beyond instilling faith in our children. Jesus told his followers, the church, to "Go therefore and make disciples. . . ." A disciple is one who has developed a close, primary relationship with the one who has

---

[*]   *Redemptoris missio*, 2.

become his teacher. Skills for forming any primary relationship are first formed for better or for worse in the family. Evangelization means trying to live our belief that the love of God and other people is what life is all about. The Christian family is in a prime position to proclaim precisely this gospel in the modern world.

In recent years several authors have written about "the Catholic moment" in the life of our nation. They affirm an opportunity for the Catholic church to lead in proclaiming and exemplifying the gospel. Families hold the prime position to proclaim the Good News of Jesus Christ as a joyful message of love, intimacy, and community if, in John Paul II's words, they become what they are. In our generation, renewal movements have helped adults and youth to become very effective evangelizers, especially as they share their stories through peer ministries such as Cursillo, Teens Encounter Christ, Engaged Encounter, Marriage Encounter, and Retrouvaille. Why couldn't such enthusiasm be generated in a parish as well?

Actions to Consider

• At The Call to Action meeting in Detroit in 1977, the statement on Family said: "We recommend that all church programs dealing with family life, at all levels, address in a special way the specific education of families in making them aware of the needs of others in their neighborhood, their local communities, or in the world community" (II, 1). If social action is experienced by youth as something their class does once a year or in a community-service course, it will probably not be included in their life agenda. But if a sense of mission is integrated into the routine of family living, then it is experienced as an integral part of life.

• Help parents teach their children the beauty and variety of the human family, the suffering of that family, and how families can alleviate suffering and restore the dignity of all God's people. Families can break down the barriers of discrimination by contact, regularly visiting a nursing home for the elderly, participating in events for the mentally handicapped, or taking part in the cultural activities of other ethnic groups. To shield children from or fail to expose them to the suffering of their brothers and sisters is to fail to offer them the depth of the Christian faith. Families may respond to the challenges of human suffering by serving in the local soup kitchen, helping the elderly shut-ins with correspondence or grocery shopping, or sponsoring an overseas child. Caring for the extended family allows grief and anger at our wounded society to flow out in acts of love and acts of resistance.

• For too long a separation has existed between the family and social action. To enable the mission, the church's social teaching must make those links between family and social action explicit. The church must continue to work for those services families need in order to survive and to move beyond survival to engage in the church's social mission. The church needs to help families see the relevance and urgency the social agenda holds for their own well-being. To invite families to see themselves as family centered churches will help them move more fully into the world rather than retreat from it.

• Parishes wisely form support groups for families involved in the mission of the church. Small communities of faith can provide the support without which families cannot sustain their involvement over the long haul. The more families connect locally and globally, the broader their vision becomes, the more joy and sense of purpose they experience, and the deeper their commitment grows.

• Family-centered religious education, popular among parishes a decade ago, appears in decline. Evidence suggests that programs best affect students when the family is considered part of the religious education team. When faith does not support home activities, many youth fall prey to a religious skepticism that grows and festers. The most successful programs involve parents sharing their faith and receiving nurturance from each other, their children, and the extended family of faith. Much of the catechesis in the home is informal, unstructured and attitudinal, yet the message does not escape children.

• Peer ministries are built on a sense of mission, of helping others in need. Any parish is rich in the experience of families, but most persons do not have confidence that they have anything to offer to others. We have done some training for Eucharistic ministers and lectors, but little for family ministers in most parishes. Training programs to work with engaged couples, hurting marriages, or any family ministry should be at least one full weekend. The length of training says a lot about the importance we assign to any ministries.

• The parish can link needs with those who have gifts to minister to those needs. Linking hurting couples with couples in recovery or experienced parents with new parents can be a great service. Couples often do not know where to turn for help. Those who can help often do not know of the needs or feel confident to offer their services. The Stephens ministry has done some of this linkage.

• As parishes develop mission statements, urge families to develop a mission statement. Many families act out of crisis and immediate needs rather than on shared vision and values. Writing a mission statement gives expression to a family's true foundation and direction. Writing a mission statement becomes a key way to improve the family and to help families "become what you are."

9

That They May Have Life

You celebrate life – birthdays and weddings, births
and deaths, a first day of school and a graduation,
rites of passage into adulthood, new jobs, old
friends, family reunions, surprise visits, holy days
and holidays. You come together when tragedy
strikes and in joyful celebration of the sacraments.
As you gather for a meal, you break bread and
share stories, becoming more fully the community
of love Jesus calls us to be.

LITURGY IS THE SACRAMENTAL SIDE OF OUR MISSION AS CHURCH.
As the bishops statement above indicates, ritual and liturgy
are essential elements of family spirituality. *It is a definite
paradigm shift to recognize that the home, not the parish, is the ordinary place for liturgy and ritual.* A family's spiritual life is defi-
nitely affected by its participation in the life of the parish. Yet
many Catholics feel cheated that what they hear in church on
Sunday morning is quite irrelevant for their life during the
week. They feel a need for affirmation and insights about life
that just don't come from the church's liturgies.

For many generations, parishes have been able to take
families for granted. Church leaders expected families to remain strong and family relationships to endure difficult times.
They expected family values would be shaped primarily by
Christian tradition and by the teachings of the church. Parish
leaders expected the support of the "good Catholic families"
they talked about while doing little to meet their needs. They
overlooked the interdependence of the family-centered church
and the parish church. The parish church, by its silence and

neglect, bears part of the responsibility for the breakdown of family life today.

Families and parishes need each other if either is to be an authentic form of church or Christian community life. Right now the responsibility falls primarily on parishes. Either parish leaders began to take serious and effective steps to nourish Christian family life or the church will be seen as even less relevant.

Vatican II failed to acknowledge the essential connection between liturgy and the life of members in society. This led to confusion after the council. Initially, liturgical reform was expected to revitalize the communal life of the church and bring about a more active sense of mission. But the liturgical reforms failed to create strong community among persons who understood being Christian as individual piety rather than community involvement. Liturgists failed to probe deep enough into the relationship which must exist between faith and life, liturgy and work or family.

Worship should help us link life and faith, throwing light on our experiences from the perspective of the Christian story and helping us appreciate the sacramentality of all experience. Worship is not for God's sake but for ours. Through worship, we acknowledge who we are and what we can become. Our worship makes no sense apart from our Christian mission. The liturgy reminds us of our election by God, plants the Word of God deeply into our hearts, and calls us to publicly affirm our resolution to carry out this mission.

In Eucharist, we celebrate our call to create a community founded on the spirit of the Gospel, acknowledging that we have a communal mission to build the Kingdom. The sacraments prepare us for this mission. Right now, the Sunday Eucharist fails to be that exciting celebration in which God is made present to the community in such a way that members go forth enriched by the good news and able see the sacramentality of all life.

Persons responsible for parish life generally believe the present model of liturgy is relevant to life experiences and effective for folks who participate. Many persons searching for meaning, however, see little reason for going to the church as they experience it. Yet ninety-nine percent of the church's money, time and energy are directed to getting them there. The place to start is with life rather than liturgy. The roots of liturgy are in society rather than in the church. Liturgy has to do with life in the world and how the common can be made holy.

Persons in the pews on Sunday morning have two principal concerns, their daily work and their family relationships. Yet these two concerns are generally neglected from the pulpit and in the liturgical message. These families are impacted more heavily by the materialism and strain of the secular world. The parish misses an opportunity here. People will continue to rate the homilies as inferior until the priest consults with the laity to understand their experiences. What now happens in the parish is more ritualism and formality.

The church is not our life but its search for meaning and inspiration. We gather to get a vision for life outside the church community. The experience gained in the assembly which breaks the Word of God and the Bread of Life is crucial to our vision. To be faithful to its mission, the church must be confronted again and again with the Word of God.

We too often view the church not as salt and leaven for the world but as a permanent retreat from life in the world, a protective fortress for its members. The Sunday assembly then fades into a daily routine of fairly constant ritual action. This is enhanced with the American experience that diversity requires religion to retreat into private. We have not yet achieved a deep sense of our union with each other in the congregation let alone with the entire society. Thus our liturgies become cozy celebrations rather than preparation to be church all week long outside the parish buildings.

We live in a society where our lives are divided into compartments, such as work, family, recreation, and faith. Each aspect of our personal life is divorced from every other and we depend on specialists who relate in increasingly narrow ways to only one part of our personal life. It is not surprising that our life of faith should be lived apart from our family life and social concern. We want the church to be concerned with our private religious life and not with the rest of our life. Most parish renewal programs are based on the assumption that a parish is a gathering of individuals whose relationship with one another is unimportant to what the parish is about.

"Every day the church gives birth to the church," says St. Bede. Is this not the goal of the parish church? Liturgy expresses our continuing efforts to be one with each other in Christ, and gives us the energy and will to carry out this effort in the midst of daily life. Liturgy celebrates our unity, our brokenness, and our desire for reconciliation with all persons. Both home and parish liturgies should touch at the heart of our lives, embracing such hopes and fears as the joy and pain of family life, the struggle for women's rights, the respect for every life, the protection of people from the faceless economic complex, the whole of our Christian story.

Those who lead our parishes are poorly equipped to nurture family life. They usually view family ministry as another program. Instead, it is a whole different way of being a parish community. Family ministry is first of all a set of values and attitudes that inform and shape every ministry in the parish. It looks at ministries as relational, nourishing those intimate relationships that form the very heart of our lives. We minister to the individual by ministering to his or her relationships with those persons he or she loves.

Signs and Symbols

1950s families knew what it meant to be Catholic. Catholics abstained from meat on Friday, did penitential acts during Lent, went to Mass and Confession and prayed the rosary. Catholic homes were easy to identify by the sick call set, pictures of the Sacred Heart and Mary, and holy water fonts. Benediction, the Blessed Sacrament, Latin Masses, Stations of the Cross, and incense made Catholic parishes distinctive. The American Catholic culture was once so powerful and unified that everybody over a certain age has almost identical memories of it.

Today's church still creates a sense of family but does not deliver one and the same experience to all its members anymore. We got rid of a lot of Catholic symbols after Vatican II without replacing them with new ones. As a result we have a less distinctive religion. Many agree that the lack of symbols in our homes and parishes contributes to the crisis of faith. Humans are symbol-makers. From the earliest moments of our consciousness, we interpret our experiences through symbols.

It is not that we have lost the sense of the symbolic and the sacramental. In part, we have lost the once clear distinction between the sacred and the secular. Many worry that society appears to be totally secular, with the loss of so many symbols we once considered sacred. We are so bombarded by the trivial made important through advertising and the daily news that our Catholic symbols of the past seem insignificant and drained of effectiveness. Some things in our life almost seem more sacred than our dehydrated sacramental symbols, such as a hard-earned varsity jacket, a driver's license, a credit card, yellow ribbons during the Gulf war, fireworks on the Fourth of July, and a torch to begin the Olympics.

Archbishop Rembert Weakland of Milwaukee said of our time, "We live in an age in which it is necessary to re-imagine American Catholicism." Religious leaders, more interested in keeping the church together by controlling the intellect and will, have lost a sense of mystery and contemplation, that essential component of religion. Today the scientific community explores the mystery of the universe while religious leaders are bent on concrete interpretations of religious events. Ordinary people recognize the mystery of every day, the transcendent nature of such ordinary events as falling in love, raising a child, or lending a supportive hand. Mystery abounds in our everyday lives when we open our eyes to it.

Faith is a quest for the spiritual meaning of our existence. Our faith is founded on the symbolical and metaphorical nature of the scriptures, e.g., the Biblical account of creation and the fall of our first parents or of the kingdom of God. Metaphor is the natural language of the interior life, of the spirit and of the soul. The scriptures portray mystery present everywhere for those who have eyes to see and ears to hear. Mystery is a discernible aura around every human event.

The demand for conformity to religious truths rather than a search for mystery works against a vital religious faith. When we stop appreciating the ambiguity and pluralism of life, we fail to comprehend the work of the Spirit. Large numbers of American Catholics have a higher degree of theological understanding than their immigrant forebearers and hope for but are despairing of receiving a deep sacramental, spiritual response to guide their journey. They look to the parish to affirm their sacramental intuitions, to recover a language of symbol and ritual, and to provide a certain wisdom regarding the paradoxical and mysterious. When the church gives quick, logical answers to the broken moments and seemingly dark alleys people encounter regularly, such superficial cliches reveal an uneasiness with the spiritual dimension. Trying to make sense out of the death of innocent children, for example, may make the person who speaks feel better but seldom touches the suffering family.

Religion does not explain life so that every little happening makes sense. Faith, and the church which symbolizes it, provides a way of looking at our world that enables the suffering and questioning to perceive the nonrational character of mystery. The church is to reveal and explore the utter mystery that lies at the very root of existence. A sacramental church, by means of metaphor and symbol, helps people penetrate the outer texture of everyday life to sense and experience the redemptive nature of life's ordinary rhythms.

There is a spiritual restlessness in American culture not met by clear, concise answers. A genuine sacramental search brings not answers but more profound questions. It gives us a rich sense that what we experience holds the mystery of God's presence. No experience is spiritually neutral. A man and woman in love sense something of a God who wants to share everything with them.

The church has constant opportunity to point symbolically to the mysterious nature of life. The sacramentality of ordinary events needs to be underscored so that people recognize that the spiritual mysteries may be celebrated when the parish gathers but are also celebrated in the seemingly homely events of daily life like rising and bedtime, family meals, birthdays and holidays. In response to the Midwest flood of 1993, we could see the goodness and generosity, the spiritual depth of ordinary people who so often said about their helping, "I had to do it." In their actions we could see more deeply into ourselves as well.

Symbols show our values and communicate messages between people. Our emotions are stirred by pictures of a warm embrace, flag burning, or police brutality. Through symbols we are able to share with one another what is inmost to our being, our consciousness. Basically, all symbols, including words, can be classified as signs that lead us to know something beyond themselves. We have, however, lost much of our religious language. Many persons show much greater fluency when talking about computer technology than when talking about religion.

Symbols differ from simple signs because they touch a deeper consciousness. They touch our imaginations, emotions, desires and loves and trigger our decisions and our activity. Any given symbol has the power to resonate with the deeper levels of our consciousness. Thus we use Hitler as a symbol of human evil and Mother Teresa as a symbol of human concern and compassion. Symbols do not merely express how we think and feel; they are a powerful force in shaping the way we think and feel.

There are moments in life that demand religious symbol and celebration. When a child is born, even parents who don't need the church demand that their baby be baptized. Two people who are vowing marriage expect the church to witness their vows even though they don't understand the commitment they are making. At the moment of death, God and church suddenly become essential. Many moments in our life, such as intimacy, parenting, forgiveness, and daily efforts to be with each other, need celebration. Families today also have great need to express in liturgy the pain of troubled teenagers, broken marriages, sickness and loss.

Sacramental thinking views reality not as a thing but as a symbol. The world, persons, even things are penetrated by God and can be a sacramental vehicle of grace. Everything is a sacrament from God's viewpoint. Daily life is full of sacraments, signs that recall and communicate another Reality.

Celebrating Sacraments

We can see how church life over the centuries broke down to become largely nonparticipatory. In no place is this more evident than in the sacraments, whose symbols no longer communicate their reality and seem barely relevant to our daily life at home and at work. We have difficulty understanding the sacramental liturgies because we do not understand the broader sacramentality of our lives as Christians.

Good worship gives expression to this sacramentality, even while allowing it to be challenged and transformed by the memory of Jesus Christ. Sacraments ritualize the acts of home, family, and of the community which transcend family ties, expressing their meaning in simple but aesthetic form, such as the breaking of a loaf of bread, the pouring of water, the sharing of a common cup, or the laying on of hands. Good rituals allow participants to see their lives reflected in the shared caring and identity, and at the same time to stand back from life and its activities in order to perceive their meaning and the larger perspective of mystery within which they belong.

In the experience of loving and being loved, we touch the God who is love. If the church is the sacrament of Christ, marriage and family life is the sacrament of the church. Family life is the church in miniature. For most persons, the experience of sacramental/spiritual life takes place within the family. Beginning with baptism and through the other sacraments, we come to know Christ in an intimate and personal way in the communion of our family. The expression of parish life and liturgy will hold little meaning for a person who finds no realistic support for such expressions within the family. If we do not have the joyful experience of communion at the family table, we will scarcely appreciate the joy of the eucharistic table. The same is true for the forgiveness and reconciliation essential for both family unity and Christian unity.

Daily life in the family helps us understand the meaning of marriage as sacrament. Members are called to be grace for each other, often truly amazing grace. Couples learn that God can be trusted to renew and heal their love each and every day, even when the going gets difficult. Love for each other brings them into union with God, and union with God brings them into intimacy with each other.

The basic attitudes of hospitality – welcome, acceptance, service, trust, and friendliness – are key to the formation of a sacramental community. The family-centered church, which knows what it means to welcome a new member, promises at baptism to guide this child through the process of faith development. The renewal of the Rite of Christian Initiation for Adults is making us more aware of the central need for a community. Both as parish and family, we live and celebrate in community, where we are called to be one and to share what we have and are.

Forgiveness is essential to family living, to healing and wholeness. Being human means having to say we're sorry and we forgive again and again. I'm sorry I hurt your feelings. I'm sorry I had to work late every night this week. I forgive you for failing to see things my way. I forgive you for what you have done to almost break up our marriage. Every experience of human forgiveness is rooted in the gratuitous forgiveness of a merciful God.

Jesus emphasized the homecoming families experience in reconciliation. He told the story of a runaway son so dissatisfied with his life that he wished his father dead so he could have his inheritance and freedom away from home. However, the prodigal son parable focuses on the father, who constantly watches for his son and for us when we've strayed far from home, who has no bitterness when we've wished him out of our lives, who recklessly runs halfway down the road to meet us when we are still far away. Too often the parish community has acted like the prodigal son's brother, sitting in judgment and refusing to celebrate when someone returns home.

Reconciliation celebrates a God who finds a way to catch our attention when we've separated ourselves. The church is to search us out and call us, perhaps during a crisis or illness or retreat. Our hearts begin to open and we find ourselves being drawn back to God. Finally letting ourselves slowly make our way back home, the sacrament of reconciliation begins when we are ready to celebrate our homecoming. It's wonderful to be back where we belong. Celebrating reconciliation, at home and in the parish, should remind us there's no place like home.

Jesus used the Passover meal, where families recalled the story of their relationship with God, as the moment for giving us the Eucharist. For the Old Testament prophets, the marriage covenant provided the symbol for God's covenant with the people. In the symbolism of the Last Supper, Jesus made this link between Eucharist and Christian marriage very apparent by using the two most central human symbols of love and concern. Jesus took the giving of food, a most basic action of parents from the time a mother nurses her child, in his use of bread and wine. He united this with the symbol of the sexual union of husband and wife as he said over the bread: "This is my body given for you."

We gather as Christians to make this story of God's interaction with humans our story by celebrating the Eucharist. Because the Christian story is about a covenant between God and us, it requires a personal decision to make it our own. We seal this covenant in the breaking of the bread and the sharing of the cup, where we bind ourselves to become with each other the one body of Christ. As we share this covenant meal, the everyday events of our lives take on a sacramental character. Little room is left for the individualistic "Jesus and me" mentality which marked our eucharistic piety when we considered the Mass a sacrifice more than a covenant meal.

Vatican II reaffirmed that the people as church are a sacrament of Christ's presence. The nature of the church is first of all sacramental. Through the living vocabulary of symbols it points to and nourishes the spiritual reality beneath the everyday world of appearances. The sacraments hallow those experiences in which we feel the presence of God in our lives.

Proclaiming the Good News

Charles Peguy once said that "The true revolutionaries in our society are the parents of Christian families." They are so uniquely different from the usual families around us that they are indeed revolutionary. Christian family life faces stressful obstacles, often alone. A parent, also a professional man, told the U.S. bishops at a hearing several years ago at Notre Dame: "The hardest task I have had as an adult is raising my children. And I can say – without blame but with intended objectivity – that the church has been of very little help."

Parish ministers may talk about the family on Mother's Day or the Feast of the Holy Family. Otherwise, most give scant time to preaching and teaching about this subject, even though American Catholics say they most need help "in my marriage and family life." We seem to shy away from family issues as too difficult to handle, turning family relations over to the guidance of secular counselors or even Dear Abby. Rather than interpreting family life prophetically, the church too often accepts the values of the local culture. If anything, the church has overlooked the family despite its rhetoric, suggesting that commitment to the Christian family is an ideal rather than a value. People think their ideals are important but lack the commitment to make ideals part of their current reality while they are willing to sacrifice now for their values. Our ideals don't shape our plans and actions, our values do. Simply put, on family matters the church does not put its energy and money where its mouth is.

Our married brothers and sisters have been hesitant to talk about the spirituality of struggling relationships, budget shortages, reconciliation, and hanging in there with teenagers because their failures seem all too evident. Yet Paul reminds us: "If I must boast, I will make a point of my weaknesses" (2 Cor. 11:30). "This treasure we possess in earthen vessels is to make clear that its surpassing power comes from God and not from us" (2 Cor 4:7). Spouses quickly admit that marriage "has its ups and downs." In down times, marriage involves a continual daily renewal of the decision to love so staggering that it can only be made through the grace of God. While our culture emphasizes what we get out of marriage and family, Paul reminds Christians that the love of husband and wife is to be modeled on the love Jesus showed us when he laid down his life for us (Eph. 5: 22-33).

It can be difficult to preach to persons in the pews, some of whom are divorced, living in shaky marriages, or struggling with teenage children. Somehow, it seems improper to discuss their needs and hurts from the pulpit. Yet scriptures remind us that God came to call sinners and to minister to those in need.

Hesitancy to preach about family concerns may also result from a failure to speak from the authority of the Bible. Pastoral people sometimes dismiss the scriptures as coming from a different era and lifestyle and having little to say about marriage today. Biblical views certainly form a striking contrast to those of our society, appearing to be "a stumbling block and an absurdity" (I Cor. 1:23). Jesus' view of the marital relationship as a lifelong and exclusive commitment ("Let no man separate what God has joined") contrasts starkly with a headline in the June, 1988 *Cosmopolitan* entitled "Why Love Is Not Built To Last."

The pastoral minister must understand the lives of families, their hopes and struggles, and the social context in which they live. People's lives are influenced and shaped by media portrayals of marriage as an antique and hopeless institution, and by media messages which evangelize far more profoundly than the gospel message.

That the pulpit should be silent in the face of such cultural messages and practices is inconceivable. To throw up our hands in surrender would be sinful neglect. Pastoral leaders must not avoid the demanding challenge to minister to a people caught in such dizzying changes as the women's movement or the abortion controversy. The gospel bears on these too.

Americans still rate family as a strong value. Our family defines who we are and what we become. Christian faith is primarily concerned with human relationships. In the scriptures, our relationship with God is never separated from our relationship with persons around us. Talking about the demand to love our neighbors, Martin Luther once pointed out that the nearest and dearest neighbor is the person with whom we live, which is where our love must begin.

Reinhold Niebuhr said that "Love involves the willingness to take responsibility." Christian home life invites a lifestyle so uniquely different from our culture's standards that it is, as we noted, truly revolutionary. When his listeners could no more accept Jesus' expectations for marriage as permanent than could the rich young man give up his riches to become a disciple, he assured them that such a challenge was impossible in human terms "but for God all things are possible" (Matthew 19:26).

The pastoral minister's call is not to proclaim the message of our culture nor personal opinions but the gospel. To do this requires listening intently to the bible to hear the living word of God. It also means listening as God speaks through people who help ministers make connections between faith and life. Right now, peer ministers in the renewal movements often speak out much stronger than pastoral ministers. Paul reminds us we are stewards of the mysteries of God. People need and want to hear the truth. No easy way exists to accomodate the world's way and the Christian way.

People who hunger for someone to preach with authority from the scriptures go away disappointed far too often. When pastoral leaders can clarify their everyday experiences by unfolding the Word of God, they react with relief and joy. Someone has finally affirmed their experience that marriage and home life, for all the trauma, are gracious gifts from a loving God. People don't expect to hear that marriage is easy. They find hope, however, when assured Easter Sunday follows Good Friday in most lives.

Persons who accept our culture's message that family concerns have nothing to do with what they believe may share communion together at Mass and yet refuse to talk at the family meal because they are in the midst of a family feud. At Mass or at family prayer each day, they may ask God to "Forgive us our trespasses as we forgive those who trespass against us," and yet nourish grudges against one another as they pass silently in the hallway. Persons in hurting marriages are more likely to ask whether they will be happier separated than to ask what is God's will for them. They can deny Jesus Christ as readily by their attitude toward a bleary-eyed spouse seated across the breakfast table as by neglect of prayer and worship. They can also serve the Lord as fully by supporting teenagers who color their hair orange and wear an earring in their search for identity as in serving the poor.

Family life becomes a way Christians witness to the good news of Jesus Christ. Although people often fail to be aware of it, their relationships at home give powerful testimony to other people. When a friend gets a divorce, we all feel threatened. When a couple celebrate a fiftieth anniversary at the parish Mass, we all feel a certain pride and hope that fidelity and permanence are indeed possible.

Somehow, people generally share little about the happiness and personal growth of their family relationships. They enjoy these satisfactions in the privacy of their home; thus silence may suggest they are not that secure in these relationships. Our world needs the witness of stable marriages and healthy families. The call to such witness seems clear: "Your light must shine before others so that they may see goodness in your acts and give praise to your heavenly Father" (Matthew 5-16). Parishes might enable this by celebrating special anniversaries or by letting family members share their experiences in parish settings.

The task of proclaiming the gospel message to families is complicated by their disbelief in the message of the institutional church. As a lot of frustrated Catholics turned their backs on the church, a growing feeling emerged that the church should stay out of the personal life of marriage. The disappointment of *Humanae Vitae* for Catholics agonizing over family planning, and the shattered hopes of divorced Catholics wanting to remarry, brought strong backlashes and cost the church credibility with the faithful. That day when the message of the teaching church was considered almost gospel is gone. If anything, a skepticism about the church's teachings regarding marriage and family prevails.

In *Divorced in America*, Joseph Epstein says that divorce trends mirror a general decline in the credibility of religion.[*] He believes that adherence to God's will kept marriage together in the past. When God is not there to judge us, and our own values become the source of defining right and wrong, then we do what we want. Today we tend to shy away from any absolutes of right and wrong, allowing individuals to define what is right for themselves. When difficulties occur for couples who no longer see their marriage as important to God, they blame each other, pull away or use other protective behaviors, or hurt in silence rather than turn to God together. Prayer, in contrast, helps us confront our dividedness as we seek to understand God's will.

---

[*]   Joseph Epstein, *Divorced in America* (New York: E. P. Dutton, 1974).

Small Is Just as Effective

Americans tend to operate from a bigger is better mentality. For instance, we judge the importance of a priest by the number of families in his parish. We work hard at big liturgies which focus on the celebration itself rather than on preparing people for their mission beyond the liturgy. Because large liturgies serve such a diversity of people and needs, we find it hard to give a specific message to anyone.

The church resembles industry in this regard. New ideas or products rarely come from the major corporations. They most often come from small businesses and corporations, who may end up selling their creative ideas to the giants. Big companies tend to send questions through repeated cycles of analyses and committee reports and to be removed from the people they serve.

A similar comparison can be made between the parish church and small Christian communities or family units. The home is an excellent location for creative Christian celebration and liturgy.

We can counteract the unimaginative large Sunday liturgies through smaller liturgical experiences that can be more focused on the needs and life of the participants, such as home Masses and celebration of special events with a group of family and friends in the parish church. Actually, the home should be the ordinary place for liturgy, with the parish church serving as the place where we gather for larger group liturgies. The home is the place for reading scripture and praying together, giving a religious tone to holiday dinners, commemorating the death of a relative, remembering a baptismal anniversary, anointing a sick member, acknowledging God's blessings, and celebrating reconciliation after conflict.

In any family celebration, the presence of a friend adds something special. Families rightly acknowledge the presence of Christ in their liturgical celebrations, a presence that was obscured when we acknowledged Christ's presence on earth primarily in the Eucharistic bread in our churches. When family members are aware of the abiding presence of Christ in their relationships with each other, life in the family potentially becomes a continuing liturgy and profession of faith as families celebrate God's call and their response, self-giving that leads to self-revelation, or suffering that leads to renewed life. Of course, the family is also present to the ideas, values and ways of the secular world that differ from gospel values. Rather than view this as a grave danger, the world can be seen as a setting for the ministry of Jesus and thus for the mission of the family.

Children need to see how the spiritual life is significant to their parents at home as well as at church. Otherwise the artificial dichotomy between faith and life that marks the modern church is reinforced and perpetuated. Children need to see their parents setting aside time for prayer, worship, reflection, and open discussion about faith issues. Parents best teach the spiritual life by modeling it.

Children need concrete objects and physical activity in learning, which makes ritual important in family worship. Rituals are embodied ways of celebrating God's presence in the midst of ordinary life. They take the common stuff of life and reveal its sacramental capacity. Family worship should always include some ritual expression rather than remain in the realm of abstract words. Adults also respond inwardly to the power of symbols and actions in worship.

Family worship gives creative expression to our life with God in the home. A family ritual can be as simple as the ancient Jewish meal blessing, in which a glass of wine or juice is blessed and passed from one family member to another, followed by bread blessed and shared in like manner. The simple act of lighting a candle can turn prayer and scripture reading into a ritual.

The living message of the scriptures can enlighten a family's story. The task for the family is to discover the Gospel message as their own by discovering Christ's love in action in their lives. Living this Gospel message within the family becomes a motivating force for reaching out to others in need. The scriptures report the story of other families who encountered tragedy but committed themselves to family life in the face of difficulties.

Marriage preparation offers a key moment for ministry within the family. This is a teachable moment, a faith moment. Growing in love may provide the first strong faith experience for a young adult. We teach children knowledge of God. Faith, however, builds on an adult experience of God, when persons reflect deeply on the questions and mysteries of life. Why do we now take marriage preparation out of the family?

Weddings offer one of the most powerful moments for ministry to the whole community. We would do well to replace many of the cultural symbols of marriage with more powerful symbols of the sacramental commitment and of the parish's covenant to support couples called to be sacraments in the community.

Parishes need strong Christian families because without them they are empty of life and meaning. Families need parishes, because no family can live the Christian life in isolation. A family may try very hard to be an authentic family-centered church. Unless the parish is truly a supporter of family life and a convener for groups of families, that family will be greatly handicapped in its efforts to pass the faith to children or to live a healthy family lifestyle. Parishes need families; families need parishes.

Actions to Consider

• Home masses offer a good opportunity to focus the liturgy on a specific event or need, gathering the extended family, neighbors and friends. Masses to celebrate leaving home or returning, safety after a crisis, engagements, anniversaries of birth, marriage or death provide a focused moment in the family setting and a chance to involve family members in planning and taking part in the liturgy.

• American Catholics say they find God most often and intimately in their family life. A church that encourages visits to the Blessed Sacrament in the parish church could also encourage visits to God's presence in the family church. Father Anthony De Mello writes of a man who, on his way to the parish church to fulfill his religious duties each day, would stop at the doorway of his house, turn and say, "Goodbye, Lord God!"

• Ed Hayes suggests that families have a sacred space in their home, a custom from earlier times. A sacred space provides a reminder that the home is sacred and that everything that takes place in it is holy. This sacred room becomes a place for meditation and prayer, a place to keep the Bible and other holy objects, including spontaneous offerings such as wildflowers, autumn leaves, a bright feather, a homemade cross, or children's art work. Such a shrine offers evidence that a family believes God is more than a Sunday experience. Hayes suggests that as we elevate the common and ordinary in life to the realm of home liturgy, we will soon invest the other activities and places in our lives with the same sense of the sacred wedded to the secular. We cannot hope to make our workplace or world or even our parishes alive with God if our homes are empty of the holy.*

• Encourage family prayer time. While prayer is an intimate conversation with God, family prayer leads also to a deeper relationship with the family and the larger community with whom we share. In the family, prayer begins informally in our intimate conversations as we share thoughts and feelings with family members. Good communication leads to a deeper communion with God as God's love is revealed to us through others. Families come together to talk about God's will in their lives and to listen as God speaks to them through each other.

• Provide families with rituals and devotions that are relatable. Children respond very well to the Advent wreath ritual, especially if practiced faithfully throughout the season. The making of special foods and colorful decorations for particular seasons of the church year can be ritualized with a few simple songs or prayers. Singing hymns or songs of faith together can provide a joyous family ritual. Blessings of a car, a home, a betrothal, a new mother, an Easter basket or a Christmas crib remind us that these things, places, or events are sacramental. Objects such as a family baptismal robe, Grandma's table cloth, an object special to a family member, or a wedding album can enrich liturgies. Family worship gives creative expression to our life with God in the home.

• It would be a blessing for the couple and for the community to get weddings back into the regular liturgical

---

* Edward Hayes, *Secular Sanctity*, (Easton, Kansas: Forest of Peace Books, Inc., 1984).

celebrations as they are in most countries. We now celebrate baptisms and confirmations at parish liturgies. A wedding at the five o'clock Mass on Saturday would take a huge burden off the couple in terms of liturgical planning, give better focus to the sacramental meaning of marriage, and emphasize this not as a moment for their personal show but for community celebration of their vocation. Weddings at parish liturgies might clarify the difference between coming to the church to get married, which may result in a civilly valid marriage only, and coming to commit themselves to live as a sacrament of the church. When we acknowledge that some weddings celebrated in our parishes were never sacramental relationships, we have a clear reminder that without God's grace our actions are prone to struggles and failure.

• People come to the parish worship already shaped by family stories, already seasoned with prayer, already seized by grace, already celebrating a liturgy. They come already touched by the holy in the ordinary or struggling to make sense of the cancer stealing their bodies. Before they ever reach the church door, they they are already celebrating what Karl Rahner calls "the liturgy of the world." Invite them to make a list of the best blessings and deepest sorrows of the week, bringing this list on Sunday so that the Mass can be a celebration of the graces and an offering of the sorrows of the week past.

• Encourage one night of the week as family night in the parish, when no parish events can be scheduled. Family nights help to promote unity and foster healthy values. Many families value time together, but the fast pace of our society often means that unless a family intentionally saves some time by putting the date on the calendar it gets squeezed out.

• One sacred and beneficial ritual we might encourage any married couple to initiate is a weekly date. Dating strengthens a couple's relationship and demonstrates their love to their children. Children need to see quality, loving relationships in a world that says family breakdown is the norm. Seeing parents anticipate time alone with a spouse and have fun together sets an example children will never forget.

10

New Wine, Old Wineskins

> An enduring marriage is more than simply endur-
> ance. It is a process of growth into an intimate
> friendship and a deepening peace. So we urge all
> couples: Renew your commitment regularly, seek
> enrichment often, and ask for pastoral and profes-
> sional help when needed.

A 1980 HARRIS POLL INDICATED THAT 96% OF AMERICANS PLACED
"having a good family life" at the top of the list of goals for
themselves. Yet a dramatic change from the American family
and the Catholic Church of the 1950s caused many to predict
the decline of both. This chapter looks at sources of energy
and hope holding promise these changes may evolve into
something nearly as good as we think family and church were
in the 1950s.

Despite all the negative warnings about the future of the
family, Ashley Montague optimistically predicted: "The very
stresses and threats of modern life outside the home – out
there in what is variously termed the lonely crowd, the as-
phalt jungle, the neon wilderness and the air-conditioned
nightmare – may have the paradoxical effect of enhancing the
attractiveness of family life as a site of enduring relationships
and an island of stability in a madly gyrating world."[*]

Consider the paradox that, despite such massive changes
as the high divorce rate and two wage earner marriages, most
people in our society still desire strong families and remain
devoted to the idealized picture of family life. Family imagery
plays a strong role in our political symbols and slogans. It

---

[*] Ashley Montague, "Can the Family Survive Free Love?," *Empire Magazine*, November 4, 1979.

permeates our deepest aspirations, fears, resentments and hopes. Even so, we make it more and more difficult for families to survive as intact, intimate units.

Families themselves add to the pressures. Eda LeShan reminds us: "Our expectations are higher than ever before. We don't want to live with anyone unless there is love – not some silly idea of romantic love, but the sort of love that nourishes the soul and enables people to grow. We seek the same kind of love in which people want more for each other than for themselves and want most of all to enhance their own lives by helping someone else become all that he or she can be."*

Perhaps the discontent with where the family is at now and the desire for what we want it to be holds the key to hope. We see more and more books and articles published on marriage and family life. A whole profession has grown up around trying to help couples achieve stability in marriage. Families are reaching out to support each other, recognizing their individual health depends upon healthy communities.

The New Face of the Church

From today's perspective, we view the 1950s church as sexist, rigid, male-dominated, paternalistic, and irrelevant; yet at the time we imaged that church as stable, embodying the truth, a trusted mother and teacher. Like many American corporations, the Catholic church seems to have alienated many customers by products that are not updated and leaders out of touch. American families feel a leadership gap and little understanding of the issues they face trying to cope with the changing times.

Laws regarding marriage stem largely from the Council of Trent, when the Roman church tried to stop the post-Reformation exodus by reasserting its authority in religious matters. Marriage was now to be contracted by exchange of vows before a priest and two other Christian witnesses. From that time on, the church controlled the life of married couples by implying that whatever the church said was without question

---

* Eda LeShan, "The Family is NOT Dead," *Woman's Day*, (August 7, 1979).

the word of God, by encouraging spouses to remain in abusive marriages. Over the centuries, many Christian writers, usually celibates, viewed sex as an enemy of spirituality and doubted the laity could have a spirituality of their own. Couples' experience and perception of marital lovemaking did not count. The consistent message of the spiritual writers was that celibacy equaled virtue while marriage was for the weak who could not live celibate lives.

Expectations rose as Vatican II's Pastoral Constitution on the Church in the Modern World and Pope John Paul II's *Familiaris Consortio* began to move us beyond the law to better understand the nature of marriage.

Fortunately, we now have married persons well trained theologically and appreciative of the spiritual depth of their own calling who are speaking and writing on marriage, family life, and sexuality. Once taught not to trust their own feelings and experience but to depend on the judgments of church officials, they are no longer willing to yield to such hierarchical power.

1950s Catholics frequently asked approval of their moral decisions. Once the "pill" became available in the early sixties, priests were besieged with requests for permission to use this form of birth control. Then a change happened. We might view that change through the eyes of the Christian Family Movement. Pat and Patty Crowley, President couple of CFM, were one of three couples appointed to Pope Paul VI's commission on Population and Birth Control. When the Crowley's asked for the experience of American couples, they received many letters from women who unloaded burdens they had carried for years. At the end of its work, the commission prepared a majority and a minority report for the pope. The majority report, which Crowley's supported, favored a change in church policy which would not regard birth control as intrinsically evil.

When Pope Paul VI issued *Humanae Vitae* in 1968, Crowleys joined the public dissent with many Catholic theologians. Several years later, Patty Crowley reported: "Cardinal Cody has never talked to us (after the dissent) and neither has Monsignor Hillenbrand (executive priest for CFM)." Couples quickly lost interest in this debate. While most did not immediately leave the church, many started forming their own consciences rather than turning to the church for permission.

Increasing numbers of well-educated American Catholics now see themselves embodying the mystery of the church in a way differing from the institutional structure. Neither rebellious nor out to overturn the institution, they are eager to apply their faith to understand marriage and life in the world. In such ordinary experiences as falling in love, raising a child, forgiving each other, and sexual lovemaking, they discover the presence of God in their lives. Deeply tied to the church as a sacramental source for support in carrying out responsibilities to their families and professions, they look for wisdom regarding the heavy moral issues of our day. Frequently not finding this guidance and support from the Sunday homilies, they form their own consciences on daily moral choices. Most view their independent and responsible decisions as growing up.

These Catholics were prepared by members of the hierarchical church in Catholic schools and by the vigorous lay movements of the 1950s and 1960s. Their deep faith and confidence will doubtless bring about transformation of church structures, while their hunger for spirituality presents a challenge to church leaders.

These people of God have no communal voice. They have taken on some leadership in the institutional church but generally preoccupy themselves with their own lives, families and occupations. While they accept the ideals preached by the church, they feel free to dissent from such official teachings as laws on birth control or divorce when these do not match their own experience or the judgment of their consciences. Most are not indifferent toward the institutional church, nor do they feel cut off from it, but they choose to live without blindly accepting its total domination.

These folks confine most of their church activities to their parishes and to the renewal movements. The parish is, in effect, their source of identity as Catholics and the place where they express their faith. Most, however, feel disappointed that their parishes deal sparsely with their spiritual growth and sustenance. Since spiritual needs are experienced at a personal level, they expect a personal response to their needs but experience the parish church responding more to the community than to the individual. With many entering interdenominational marriages, where churches minister even less effectively, a sense of Catholic identity is at risk for a big segment of the church.

The people of God possess a common sense about moral matters, affirmed by Vatican II as the *Sensus Fidelium.* They believe the institutional church exists for them rather than they for the institution. Finding their basic faith experiences in the course of their daily lives, they look to the church to help interpret the spiritual meaning of these experiences. When the church seems more intent on disciplinary actions, they feel cheated.

Feminist consciousness has brought new meaning and relevance to women's lives. Many now refuse the dualistic and patriarchal structures, attitudes and values of the church. The women's movement is reshaping personal and professional relationships between men and women. A number of women are now moving away from a patriarchal church which refuses them full participation. Those who remain do not necessarily continue as Catholics on the terms of the institutional church, but stay for the sacraments and community they find in their parish. They feel they are as much the church as anyone and resent being talked down to by the hierarchy.

The division between the institution and the people of God is most notable over issues connected with human intimacy. The way the institution interprets sexuality in marriage, the relationship between sexes, and the nature of reciprocal marital responsibilities seems to married Catholics to be further and further removed from their experiences. People find it hard to listen to those who seem to sit in judgment and tell them how they should feel rather than listen and understand their lives.

The people of God now see themselves as adults, less dependent on the institution. American Catholics believe they are becoming more church all the time even though moving further from the institution, whose leaders speak with less authority to their lives every day. The sacramental, far more than the administrative, responses of the church provide the spiritual energy that flows from the institution into its members. While they will not listen to leaders who stress institutional loyalty above all else, they love their faith and will confer authority on those leaders who can open their eyes to the spiritual dimensions of their ordinary experiences. The shape of the new church is steadily emerging from the ground up.

Male and Female Spiritualities

Much has been written about the differences between men and women. One of the great graces and energies of our day lies in the quest for a male spirituality and a female spirituality. Rather than perpetuating the dualism that has so marred the church, a spirituality focused on being masculine or feminine will recognize that men and women are full equals. This equality honors the "male and female God created" of Genesis.

These spiritualities should not set men over against women. From the outset, they distinquish only to unite. Separatist efforts only add to the dangers of misunderstanding and dominance. Sexism is an expression of broken mutuality between women and men.

Church spirituality in the past was neither masculine nor feminine but neuter. It understood everything from the perspective of what church leaders called reason, logic, and truth. A truly masculine or feminine spirituality will be charged, alive, reciprocal, passing through stages of union, grief and every emotion in between. It cannot be managed ahead of time by rules that always work, but will require daily listening, engagement, and letting go.

Women's spirituality has made great strides by its insistence on experience rather than universal expectations or sexual stereotypes. Women until recently were reticent to trust their own experience in a male-dominated church. Now they have opened to new images and understanding of God. At the center of any spirituality is the image we have of the sacred. How we name God shapes the way we think of ourselves as created in the divine image and how we relate to God in prayer and action. One gift of the women's spirituality movement lies in its challenge to avoid making an ideal of any single way of naming the holy. We now use many images for God because none exhausts the mystery. If we are all created in the likeness of God, the images with which we point to the divine must reflect us all. No single image can do this.

Past patterns of holiness were built on stereotypes, and we still live out of many of those divisions between body and spirit, mind and emotions, care of self and care of others. Women's spirituality strives to heal the connections in a fractured world. It is concerned about creating a kind of wholeness that allows all human beings to experience the fullness of their humanity. Women have always been concerned about the body and nature. Their experiences in giving birth and raising children have brought them close to the earth and shown what it means to nurture life on all levels. Women who have suffered oppression, low self-esteem, or paralyzing fears, and now allow themselves to be touched by God, experience healing and are able to begin the journey to wholeness.

Male spirituality is indebted to the women's movement for forcing men to encounter their own "feminine." The institutional church acts in an analytical, "masculine" way toward both male and female members. In contrast, it expects members of both sexes to respond in an almost exclusively "feminine," submissive way. Once the male has been civilized by establishing a healthy relationship with his own "feminine," he has to go back and re-establish his relationship with his maleness, with what Robert Bly calls his "Wildman." The male soul thrives on challenge, the heroic, the wild, the individuated, all qualities not expected in Catholic males in the pew or in the pulpit.

Richard Rohr believes the fundamental reason men and women fail to love and to trust their masculine energy is because they suffer from a "father wound." These persons have never been deeply touched by their human father, who lacked time, freedom, or need to touch them. Men who are ashamed and mistrustful of their maleness do not provide good role models; thus their children have no masculine energy. These children become compulsive, frenetic, busy, wild in a bad sense, and ultimately seek power, sex and money.

Men in our culture have a difficult time sharing at deep levels, soul to soul. They are inhibited by a social bias against men displaying emotion or revealing their inmost thoughts and feelings. Society at large tends to define a man in terms of his job. His identity comes also from the media, which projects athletic abilities, looks, ease with women, and competitiveness as male qualities. Little in the public image allows men to be interior, tender, and able to identify with society's losers.

Masculine spiritualilty emphasizes that doing, or acting, is the primary way of developing a spirituality. The feminine is more comfortable with the interior, the soul; the masculine is more comfortable with the exterior world. Feminine spirituality includes the freedom inside to be tender, nurturing, forgiving, to let go and to surrender. The feminine is characterized by the freedom to weep and to touch. Our modern patriarchal culture does much to encourage women to be masculine in the sense of acting, achieving, and performing in the outer world, but it leaves out the reflective element. A masculine spirituality will emphasize certain human qualities as essential, a feminine spirituality will emphasize others. We need to emphasize both the masculine and feminine elements of a person's life, i.e., action and reflection, for a person to be whole.

Male or female spirituality has a close connection with male or female sexuality. Men, for example, find themselves yearning for emotional intimacy with other males. Yet they find themselves unprepared and fearful of such intimacy. They also want relationships of genuine equality and mutuality with women, yet find themselves crippled by centuries of male sexism and by emotional dependency on the opposite sex. Male or female spirituality helps us view sexuality more positively, as relational and rooted in the core of a person's self, and moves away from concentration on the individual sexual acts.

One of the important strands in the malaise between the sexes is our legacy of mistrust. This legacy owes much to the spiritual writers who depicted women as the main dangers to men's religious fidelity. Christian tradition helped sour what ought to be mutual delight between men and women.

In the struggle to develop a male and a female spirituality, two trends are to see that men and women do have an innate hunger for God, even though the churches seem to consider spirituality something for women, and that spirituality needs to be broken out of isolation and connected to every important aspect of a person's life.

Families and Renewal Movements

The renewal movements provide one of the most visible examples of a developing lay spirituality, reflecting a new understanding of the church. Movements start at the fringe, but must soon either interact with the wider church and move to its heart or they move out to become sects and usually die. What characteristics of the renewal movements make them a source of energy and hope?

The renewal movements move from an "I"-centered focus to a "We"-centered emphasis on community. The marriage and family movements, such as Marriage Encounter, Retorno, and Retrouvaille, emphasize the family-centered church and then the larger church, generating small Christian communities in contrast to today's megaparishes. In this move toward community, the clergy-laity dichotomy is weakened as clergy and laity share their lives together. A deep bond quickly builds as participants share their stories in a common shared experience which, while personal, is not individual.

Rather than building on a set of dogmas, renewal movements take a deeper look at people's own experience of God in their lives. Members' stories reveal how God continues to be present to them. We come to God through the human. Members share stories so that others may recognize their own pilgrimage and say "That's my story, too!" Robert McAfee Brown says of stories: "Finally what may happen is that hearing another story can force us to tell our own story in a different way, transformed to such a degree that we can properly call the experience one of conversion." Perhaps the current hunger to understand human experience explains the success of the renewal movements. It helps that people's experiences are finally considered important enough to share at a time when a leery attitude prevails toward all authority, including the teaching authority.

Renewal movements emphasize the importance of every person. All are called to holiness. Laity, as church, also have charisms and a right to speak and use their gifts. These peer ministries stress the equality of men and women. A substantial part of the current leadership in our parishes has been developed by the renewal movements. Yet, because they usually are not parish-based nor directly accountable to parish leaders, staffs have generally not received and supported them very well.

The movements move away from doctrinal orthodoxy and intellectual truths alone to take people where they are at and give shape to their religious thought and practice in light of their life. People are challenged to love rather than leave the world. Right relationships, whether with one's spouse in marriage or with the material universe, leave one free to enter into prayer, community, and reconciliation.

The movements mark a striking shift from a negative to a positive theology. They emphasize self-love and self-acceptance, along with a strong conversion experience and a commitment to Christ. Acknowledging the pain or paschal mystery in our lives, they see Jesus calling us to find our humanness and be fully alive; thus the conversion experience has a resurrection quality that is joyous and triumphant.

Renewal movements stress the Christian's vocational call from God to love and serve each other and to build the kingdom of God. Laity are called to minister through their daily lives. This vocational call is not a private call but a sacramental call to belong to the faithful. Marriage Encounter stresses living marriage in God's plan as a sacrament for the church. Renewal theology clearly reflects the current interest in evangelization. Examples abound of conversions among the indifferent and unchurched.

One might question whether this conversion experience lasts for most individuals. Indications of authentic conversion are apparent in a University of California study showing that Catholic Engaged Encounter makes a change in a couple's values that will last a lifetime. Persons who participated in the renewal movements in the 1970s still persevere in church leadership. Can these movements bring life back into a church that at times has been thought to be only a corpse? Perhaps!

Right now they find it difficult to recruit participants when many Catholics are walking away from the church. Yet they foster a maturity and positive spirituality not found in large segments of the church.

The renewal movements may not have a long life if the entire church does some catching up on spirituality and reduces the need for movements not directly related to parish and diocesan structures. In the meantime, they have made a definite contribution to the life of the church and to affirmation of the sacrament of marriage and family life. Thus far the attitude of the official church has been at best a wait and see stance or even less trusting. Fortunately, the renewal movements can be more flexible than the structured church. Perhaps the best we could hope for now is a good relationship where the renewal movements can thrive in the midst of the church. More biblically and creation-centered in their spirituality than the church out of which they have emerged, they offer some promise of a dynamic, gospel-based discipleship.

Healing Ministries and Self-Help Programs

At this time of brokenness and hurt, some healing ministries give hope for a better future. Beyond a doubt, one of the most important events of our century was the emergence of Alcoholics Anonymous, with the publication of the Twelve Steps in 1934. In a world of shattered families and lack of close relationships, Alcoholics Anonymous reminded us again of the need we have for each other. Twelve Step participants come together out of weakness, not out of strength, and acknowledge their personal need for God. Twelve Step programs have helped millions of alcoholics, drug abusers, gamblers, child abusers, sex offenders, and chronic victims turn their lives around to become productive, self-fulfilled individuals.

The Twelve Step programs use the original dynamic of church. Church happens when persons who have heard about Jesus' vision for life come together to share stories of their own experiences of living that vision, when those who are aware of their need for conversion gather with others to work at ongoing conversion. The church originally relied on group support and shared personal experiences at meetings, along with daily awareness of God's presence and regular contact among members.

We now realize that all addictive/obsessive behaviors affect the spouse and children of the addict as well. Because the family functions as a unit, the disease of one member creates a relationship of codependency in which family members exhibit symptoms of dysfunction. Abusive families cause members to repress their feelings and to live in silence or rage. Less than whole people entrap each other rather than build healthy relationships. Parents often reenact their own original pain on their children.

Resentment, a desire to get even with someone we feel has hurt us, alienates family members and disables them to adapt in healthy ways. It breaks down trust and intimacy. Ultimately, resentment leads us to the irrational conviction that if only other family members would change, the marriage or family would be alright. Individuals in a troubled marriage or family need a way to openly and honestly examine the true nature of their relationships and to discern changes that will bring healing. Persons need to heal themselves before they can heal their relationships. Such peer ministry groups as Troubled Couples Anonymous, using the twelve step approach, are bringing recovery and healing to many couples today.

We Saved Our Marriage (WESOM), is a twelve step program for married individuals and couples whose marriages have been harmed by an adulterous affair. Liz Brzeczek, who along with her husband, Dick, formed WESOM, says: "These people needed somewhere they could feel comfortable discussing an uncomfortable situation. They needed help and guidance to learn how to deal with their pain and all their negative emotions, then to be able to go on and heal themselves and their marriages, if that was what they wanted. For those individuals whose marriages were beyond saving, for whatever reason, WESOM would provide the emotional support necessary to pick up their lives, heal themselves, and then go on."*

---

* Richard and Elizabeth Brzeczek and Sharon DeVita, *Addicted to Adultery* (New York: Bantam Books, 1989), p. 156.

Retrouvaille, a peer ministry providing help for couples in marital trouble, places a strong focus on relationship as well as personal growth and healing through a weekend and three month follow-up. Team couples share their stories of brokenness and hurt to allow participants to acknowledge that they, too, struggle with misery and brokeness in need of healing.

Everyone would acknowledge that the divorce rate is high among couples coming from abusive dysfunctional families. As a church, we have done little to enable healing with the family of origin prior to marriage. Then we watch spouses bring all this baggage to their marriage, repeat the family behavior of abuse and shame, often fail in their marriage, and pass the burden on to their children. Family dysfunction is a multigenerational disease. Healing to break the family chain is part of the spiritual journey to wholeness. It makes much more sense to spend time with persons prior to a marriage than on annulments.

Many persons have tried hard to survive in marriage, only to find their world crashing down on them with a divorce. When these folks turned to the church in the past, they often found little help or, even worse, found new guilt heaped upon their already troubled minds. Beginning Experience for the divorced, separated, and widowed helps individuals to deal with their grief and crisis, including the feeling of being separated from their church. Using small support groups and a weekend program, peer ministers in Beginning Experience have helped many to bring some closure to the past, reconcile themselves, feel a resurrection in their lives which offers assurance they can make a new beginning, and find a sense of a caring community.

Divorce is hard on the spouses, but even harder on any children involved. Yet we seldom ask children how they feel about what has happened, more likely encouraging them to be strong for their parents. Without help through the grieving process, these children are prime targets for school difficulties, delinquency, and addictions. Rainbows for All God's Children and related programs for older children give them an opportunity to realize that they are not alone, that all their feelings are appropriate, that there are caring people willing to be with them while they grieve, and that there is an ending

point. Peers and adults working with these programs are healers who help youngsters meet the challenges of life head-on, deal
with them appropriately, and move on to healthy lives.

Henri Nouwen reminded us of the gift of "wounded
healers." Success of these healing programs comes through
persons who can share their personal stories of pain and brokenness to help others. They offer hope as they share intimate
and deep hurts, reconciliation and healing, which give participants courage to express some of their own pain. The church
would offer a great gift by being more involved in domestic
abuse programs, parent-child conflicts, and the whole range of
relationships where families need healing.

Such healing ministry finds roots and barriers in the
church. The gospel obviously stresses healing. Yet the
church's ascetical spirituality supported stoic denial of pain,
acceptance of suffering as a means of redemption, and many
messages that work against a spirit of healing. Moreover,
some of the biggest hurts that need healing occur within the
church itself. A hierarchical church is not good at healing the
hurts caused by insensitive pastors, harsh rules, and lack of
sensitivity to the individual. Most alienated Catholics can tell
exactly who hurt them. People are more ready to forgive the
church than the church is ready to recognize its failures and to
ask forgiveness for cases of abuse and neglect. Most of the
ministries listed here do ask forgiveness for the church's hurts.
Because of this, they offer hope for healing in both the family-
centered church and the hierarchical church.

Persons who participate in Twelve Step programs often
find it difficult to continue church involvement because the
program gives them an experience of warm welcome and a
true spirituality they have never been able to find in their parishes. They come to expect straightforward honesty, open
communication about issues, intimacy among members and
mutual support. What they expected in the parish happens
instead in these small communities.

Minority Cultural Experiences

Our Jewish ancestors had a deep sense of a unique call to
be God's own people. The Old Testament is filled with the

sense of the covenant God had made with the Jewish people and how they in turn lived out their part in the covenant. One's entire life was centered on this relationship with a God who as creator and loving parent rejoiced in their human lives. As a people who lived close to the soil, they found the spiritual in the sun, earth, water, babies, dancing and singing. In today's society, where fathers have been absent from the home, Jewish tradition concerning the responsibilities of fatherhood can add greatly to the image of the family we are trying to construct in America.

European Christians, raised with a spirituality involving flight from nature, bodies and sensuality, can learn a lot from the spirituality of their brothers and sisters of other ethnic backgrounds, which builds on the best of the past while also affirming the ordinary reality of this world, its beauty, and the continuation of God's holy creation here and now in a community of justice and love. Living in a highly technological society tends to blunt our sensitivity to the natural rhythms of life.

Although sometimes labelled as "pagan" by European missionaries, Native American spirituality reflects authentic gospel values. At the heart of Native American spirituality is an insistence on sharing, on being hospitable, on welcoming others. The Indian way means that when someone comes to visit, you give them a gift in appreciation that they came. In giving, persons become part of each other, a part of the sacred circle.

Native Americans always considered creation a gift from the Creator to be respected as a friend and teacher. The Creator gives all life connectedness. People are connected to the earth, which God created to support life. Contrast, for example, women's puberty rites of Native Americans, which celebrate the sanctity of the gift of producing new life, with a statement of the future Pope Innocent III: "Who can ignore the fact that the conjugal union never occurs without the itching of the flesh, the fermentation of desire and the stench of lust?"

Black Americans, too, can teach us a lot about spirituality. While European spirituality was skeptical of emotion, Blacks easily express their feelings in celebration and affirmation of God. A people in exile, their worship affirms that life does have a purpose because it is held by God, who gives strength to endure oppression and is able to bring victory out of defeat.

The content of Black prayer is set by the social conditions around them. Praise and thanksgiving are prominent, as is repentance for failures and very specific petitions. Events of life like birth, death, puberty, fertility, harvest, famine, marriage, and tragedy are expressed in religious rites. Their spiritual music preserves tradition, feeling deeply the slaves' cries for freedom.

Hispanic Catholics have blessed us with counter-cultural values such as devotion to family, gratitude and love of life, a sense of community, and priority of relationships over producing and possessing. Their festivals, dance, drama, paintings, sculpture, banners, pilgrimages, prayers and cultural rituals are unique. We can learn from what these people say and do when they experience such peaks and valleys of life as birth, the first steps and words of a child, the beginning of schooling, the passage to maturity, initiation into community, the beginning of work, marriage, parenthood, dealing with sickness, loss of a job or spouse, death, reconciliation and changes in their life.

Hispanics developed powerful oral cultures, handing on their ideals and values by stories, often accompanied by gestures, dress, food, and even dance, so that elaborate rites evolved. Thus they express their unity with all of creation, not to exploit it for power and wealth, but to reverence and appreciate it. Spanish missionaries stressed doctrine, but these folks kept their religious customs, rooting their faith in culture. Unfortunately, we do not always welcome their cultural enrichment, sometimes viewing popular devotions like votive lights, novenas, feasts, anniversaries, processions and ceremonies as superstitious.

Hispanics have a great love and respect for their elders. Two or three generations live together in the same home. Hispanic adults love and take pride in children. Children learn to listen and speak to their relatives with respect, and to offer them service. The elders, especially the grandmother, possess the art of telling stories, legends, and traditions, through which they transmit their customs and piety.

Hispanics love to celebrate, especially the reception of the sacraments. Even poor families make elaborate preparations. The social aspect of the sacraments holds great importance. Godparents are carefully selected for each sacrament, since they will be considered a part of the family. Family meals are also important, with all members of the family expected to be present. Business deals are concluded and friendship expressed by sharing food and drink.

Vatican II called for a greater acceptance of diversity. The institutional church stresses conformity, often finding it difficult to see how diversity enriches. We are called to celebrate in community as do our Hispanic brothers and sisters. We are called to the gifts of resiliency and urgency for justice of America's blacks. We are to share the inner peace so reflective of Asian Americans. We need to live in harmony with the earth as do the Native Americans. These brothers and sisters offer rich treasures of faith and ritual when we come together as the diverse but one Body of Christ.

Major Changes Needed

In 1957, Harvard University Professor Pitrim Sorokin predicted:

> [The] family as a sacred union of husband and wife, of parents and children will continue to disintegrate. Divorces and separations will increase until any profound difference between socially sanctioned marriage and illicit sex-relationship disappears. Children will be separated earlier and earlier from parents. The main sociocultural functions of the family will further decrease until the family becomes a mere incidental cohabitation of male and female while the home will become a mere incidental parking place mainly for sex-relationships.[*]

Professor Sorokin's predictions seem to be on target to date, but does this mean the trend is irreversible? Is the family truly an endangered species? The story of the Christian

---

[*] *Social and Cultural Dynamics: A Study of Change in Major Systems of Art, Truth, Ethics, Law, and Social Responsibility,* (1957).

Family Movement, whose demise could appear to support the professor's prediction, provides another perspective.

Although CFM declined in membership and enthusiasm, it was and is a powerful influence in the Catholic church. Members promoted an understanding of family life more than a decade before the institutional church developed programs. CFMers in many parts of the nation established premarriage and parent education programs and initiated family life conferences in parishes. The CFM approach of observe-judge-act was a revolution in religious education, one we now see used in the small Christian communities. CFM laid the foundation for a lived theology, tying spiritual life to daily life. Spouses working together for relationship and social change brought about a dynamic breakthrough in the model of sacramental marriage. Couples, joining for a sense of community, found themselves deeply involved in politics, education, and workplace issues for which they were ill-prepared by the church and which sometimes gained them such labels as "subversive" and "communist." We recognize today that CFM anticipated by thirty years the role of the laity as the church now understands it.

Has the influence of CFM diminished with declining membership? Hardly. It trained people for ministry. Members got heavily involved in parish life and diocesan activities, providing the leadership for many parishes. CFM gave birth to Marriage Encounter. The theology of the Mystical Body, which Monsignor Reynold Hillenbrand drummed into the hearts and minds of CFMers, helped lay leaders understand they were the church. CFM still serves as a good model for the peer support groups which families need today.

Changing times often spawn paradigmatic changes. CFM certainly modeled a sense of church as the people of God, whose members learned the gospel from their peers and then brought the gospel message to others. CFM helped identify a new role for the laity. Where these radical paradigm shifts are taking us is still not clear. Our understanding of marriage now reflects a growing awareness that life itself is relational and dynamically interconnected, which was lacking in the institutional perspective.

Family ministry is undergoing a change from programs lead by experts to peer ministry, a recognition that the real experts are spouses and family members. The family life director, a fairly new ministry position in the church, is best not a program director but a coordinator and promoter of what is already going on in families. Preventive programs, centered on the family rather than the individual and based on family strengths, deserve center stage. The proposed emphasis on a family perspective for all church ministry signals hope, as does the growing emphasis on healing rather than education in adult programs.

Powerful outside pressures fragment the family so that each member goes his or her own way and the home is only a temporary stopping point between lives that are basically unconnected. The family may deal with this situation by surrendering to the powerful social forces of our day, by creating a separate culture with as little influence from society as possible, or by entering into a process of discussion and partnership to stengthen the family's condition. The third alternative offers the best hope, but cannot be sustained by the family alone. The church will be very important as the context for discussion, decision, and commitment. Families need the church to support the idea of Christian marriage, which involves sacrifice for others, commitment, and other values not central to our culture.

We see some changes now treating the family as a partner rather than as a recipient of programs. *Our paradigm is shifting from the institution ministering to families to families and small Christian communities educating and activating members to live out the gospel in their own environment.* The family will survive, but the health of any society depends largely upon the health of its families. Imagine what might happen if all the family critics and analysts turned into advocates!

Actions to Consider

• Every parish cares about preserving family life. However, attempts to stabilize people by control over their lives, by teaching authority, or by hanging onto tradition find people walking away from this control. People need help to discuss moral issues in the light of their faith experiences rather than simple moral absolutes.

• A parish might present a series on male-female spirituality. People are searching for a spiritual life fitting their experience. Such spirituality is not about worthiness but about grace.

• Devote energy to the renewal movements, which are not parish based but a blessing to parishioners. Parishes can be partners with the renewal movements by helping recruit peer ministers, by advertising, and by offering parish facilities for these ministries.

• One weekend with a renewal movement often does more for the spiritual life of a person than 52 Sunday liturgies. These ministries suffer from lack of priests to help as presentors. Ask your parish council to let their pastor give a weekend annually, even if it means parishioners have to conduct a paraliturgy because no other priest is available.

• The church is about healing. The healing ministries offer potential for the local parish to help heal its members. Support groups based on the twelve step program can be parish based. Others, like Beginning Experience or Rainbows for All God's Children, depend upon the parish to make members aware of their existence.

• Most parishes have minority members who could teach all of us a lot. We are enriched by learning from each other. Invite minority persons to share about their home life and family rituals.

11

As the Family Goes . . .

Wherever a family exists, and love still moves
through its members, grace is present. Nothing –
not even divorce or death – can place limits upon
God's gracious love.

. . . SO GOES THE CHURCH. FAMILY MINISTRY IS BOTH A TOP
priority and a tough challenge for parish workers. A focus on
the family in parish ministry will not only enrich family life,
but will also enhance the quality of parish ministry. The following steps, not necessarily listed in order of priority, will
benefit both the family and the parish.

1. *The family needs to be understood and treated as a central embodiment of the church.* Such recognition encourages the family
to look not only without but within itself for strength and support in its religious life and in discerning its mission. Until
recently, we thought of the family as the receiver of the spiritual riches of the wider church. Members went to church to
find God and the parish became the focal point for their faith
activity. If we now acknowledge the family as the foundational place of spiritual formation, parishes will need to take
the role and support of the family far more seriously.

The parish is intended to be a gathering place, not a substitute, for the family-centered church. The family needs the
parish to shape the common beliefs and visions that help it to
be a healthy family. Likewise, the parish needs healthy families, since the quality of community, worship, Christian education, and apostolic service expressed by the parish is directly
related to the quality of our household life.

Therefore, it is in the best interest of the parish to support and nurture family life. In *Familiaris Consortio*, John Paul

II said all pastoral work must consider the family (FC, 70). What we now call a "family perspective" asks us to recognize that all parish programs and services impact family life, and to plan all church activities through the lens of the family.

Ministries in the United States have been oriented toward individuals or toward community. Because we have not understood family systems and not ministered to the family as a unit, we have fragmented family life. A family perspective tries to encourage family members to become more active as partners in choosing, shaping, and monitoring those programs and services which impact on them, especially with those institutions which increasingly share the roles, functions and responsibilities which formerly belonged primarily or exclusively to the family itself. If the parish can work from a better understanding of the day-to-day realities of family life, families will be more likely to put a greater stake in their parish.

Therefore, a family perspective requires a slow and steady shift of posture toward a renewed partnership with household life in existing parish programs rather than creation of many new programs. Otherwise the parish competes with households for their time, energy, and space, and staff become frustrated when folks don't show up for their programs. Family ministry needs to be judged not by what happens specifically under parish auspices but by what happens in the home. Too often parish programs imply that contemporary families need fixing by the church or the professionals. Any sense that the parish knows what is best for domestic life disempowers the family.

Both the institutional church and the family-centered church need to recapture the vision of the Christian family as a sacred community. Families are the basic nurturing forces for society; yet they are so stressed out now that many have all they can do to get to Mass on Sundays. Families need encouragement to spend more time together. A family perspective calls us to view the family not from a consumer mentality but from its potential as a cooperative unit of ministry and mission.

2. *Acknowledging that the people are the church, recognize the rights of Catholics to organize the ministries they need.* These

rights derive from baptism and membership in the Christian community. Catholic tradition recognizes that all members cooperate in building up the body of Christ, each in accord with their own condition and function. The church as a spiritual community is essentially a voluntary organization, intended to be paradigmatic of authentic community as a free and participatory society. Despite organizational structure, Catholics remain free to form new voluntary communities and associations to express social needs and visions. These voluntary organizations manifest the ongoing presence of the Spirit in the church, which is renewed when it welcomes their creative work into its ongoing life.

Rights, of course, exist only in conjunction with corresponding responsibilities. American Catholics are a highly educated, gifted people. As much wisdom exists at the grassroots level as at the institutional level today. Most of the changes in the church will occur at the grassroots level as Catholic laity take more responsibility for their needs and services. Church law promises Catholics a right to ask for the services they believe they need from the parish or diocese, and to advise pastors regarding the good of the church. Too often such pleas have fallen on deaf ears.

For example, some dioceses are now trimming their budgets by reducing ministries staffs even though administrative staffs continue to grow. A number of dioceses have dropped their family life office. If people believe this is an important ministry of the diocese and they cannot get the office reinstated, they have a right to look for alternatives to serve the needs of families. This might mean contracting out such services as training couples to do marriage preparation or to provide for marriage enrichment. This could be done through sponsorship by participating parishes or by selling family life services to the parishes. Many parishes, similarly, fail to provide the family ministries people expect, such as marriage counseling or support for parents. All Catholics have a right to exercise ministries for which they are properly prepared and to which the community calls them.

Church law guarantees all Catholics the right to participate in the church's mission. Catholic families have a right to establish services on their own if the parish fails to provide them. They might withhold parish support and give part of their contribution to services which they believe essential to family stability. They might set up support groups without waiting for the parish leadership to initiate these groups, even publicizing the availability of such peer ministry. They certainly have a right to dissent to parish priorities. In internal matters, the church has danced around the issue of dissent, even though U.S. bishops guaranteed such dissent in the public arena: "In our democratic society, the fundamental right of dissent cannot be denied, nor is rational debate on [policy decisions] to be discouraged."* Vatican II and the Code of Canon Law point to a collegial model for the church.

3. *Listening is essential to family ministry.* The first of four principles defined in the U.S. Catholic Bishops' *Plan of Pastoral Action for Family Ministry* is "awareness that understands." Since Vatican II, listening is a vital part of being church, although many wonder in trying times if they should not go back to a more authoritarian approach to ministry.

We listen to families for several important reasons. Families have deep values and traditions on which they believe family ministry should be based. They already listen to and care for each other and have a perspective intrinsic to family ministry. Listening helps to discern the strengths, gifts, and needs of families when the right questions are asked. Listening helps not only parish staff and volunteers but families themselves to realize the diversity of families and family values. Otherwise we tend to think of the family in terms of the nuclear family or of families active in the parish, with limited awareness of single-parent homes, the aging, families in crisis, or alienated Catholics. To build family ministry on the strengths and needs of families, we seek to minister to families where they are at and not where we would like them to be. Listening also helps surface leaders to help with family ministry.

Many families believe the church does not understand their problems. A 1989 study by Fr. Steven Preister found that even problem free families who felt fairly positive about their

---

* *On Human Life In Our Day.*

relationship with the parish reported that parish ministries used by their families were not very relevant to their family needs. Yet many of these parishes had large numbers and kinds of programs. Most of the families in the study did not know about the existence of parish family programs. They did not utilize them very much and they found those they utilized not very helpful to the serious issues they face every day.*

Similarly, a 1983 Notre Dame study by Leege and Gremillion found that almost half the parishioners in their study wished that parishes provided professional services to help deal with major family problems, particularly services addressed to marital problems and problems with alcohol or financial stress. Since these services are not available in or through their parishes, most American Catholics do not turn to the church for assistance with their family problems but turn to professionals outside the church. The Notre Dame study concluded: ". . . It almost seems as though parishioners are saying: 'the parish is the right place to set our marriages on course and to make modest adjustments in marital communication, but it has little to offer when we face truly difficult situations in our marriage . . . We wish the parishes offered more to ride out the tough situations such as severe . . . family problems.'"**

Awareness raising can bridge the clutter and chaos of everyday family life with the spiritual endeavors of the parish. Parish staffs will come to understand the craziness of home life. It allows us to formulate family ministry from the inside out, from the distinctive vantage point of family functions and relationships so that we locate the family at the center of family ministry.

Families need to be affirmed for what they are already doing and invited to move on to new and broader dimensions of ministry. To be sure, at their best families may only approach the ideal the church holds for family life and often fall

---

* Steven Priester and Sister Ann Patrick Conrad, "Catholic Families and Their Parishes," *Social Thought,* Vol. 16, No. 2, 1990, p. 90.
** Leege, D. C. and Gremillion, J., *The U.S. Catholic Parish Twenty Years After Vatican II,* (Notre Dame University Study of Catholic Parish Life, December, 1984).

very short of it. But perhaps they come closer than we think more often that we realize. What they need is a word from the church that interprets what it means to live within the family and how God transforms their natural love into the image of God's own love.

4. *Sex is as vitally important to the vocation of marriage as Eucharist is to membership in the church community.* Married couples frequently find that much of their appreciation of sex and its role in marriage runs contrary to the dominant treatment of sex in Christian tradition and the teaching of their parish. Marriage is a distinctive path for living out one's spirituality. Sex in marriage means procreation, but pleasurable sex also creates imtimacy, builds companionship, and inspires bonding. In our world of sexual confusion, the church's message needs to confirm sexuality as part of the vocational call of marriage.

We can no longer afford to separate the spiritual and the material in our lives. Sexual lovemaking is central to marriage. Good families are firmly based on good sexual relations between the spouses. Making love with one another gives spouses strength to be good parents. Good sexuality is nourishing. Desire to be with the beloved makes one feel more real, more alive, more loving, more at peace with oneself – spiritual qualities for which all humans hunger. All love puts us in touch with the divine presence, for which we have an innate hunger.

For many persons the experience of orgasm in loving marriage is the clearest experience of the divine they have ever known. When husband and wife make love, they touch the God present in each other. The church understands sexuality as central to the sacramentality of marriage. Sexual intercourse is the primary symbol embodying in a real way the entire meaning of sacramental marriage. Sacramental symbols cause what they signify, and sexual intercourse is an important way of creating, nurturing, and multiplying the love and bonding between spouses. Sexual lovemaking makes a couple more pliable of will, more prone to make sacrifices, more able to forgive and to let the other be first.

As truly symbolic of marital love, marital sex becomes a school for love. It teaches us that only by risking our whole self do we receive the whole of the other as gift. Then we are rewarded not only by physical pleasure but with intimacy that offers us closeness, communion, stimulation, and companionship. In a grace-filled marriage, couples who have grown more loving through lovemaking don't stop with their family. Their love extends outward to giving of their time, effort, love and trust to others, such as friends, children, neighbors, and the wider community. Being in touch with the God within oneself and the God within another moves us in the direction of spiritual growth.

Conveying a healthy understanding of sexuality is one of our greatest challenges as church today. Sex and sexual pleasure are so important to marriage that we should take every care to prepare persons to be good lovers of their spouses. The sacramental status of marriage puts much of the responsibility for such preparation on the church. Marriage preparation programs do not deal adequately with sexuality. The church could improve marriage preparation by supporting comprehensive sexual education programs in public and parochial schools. Using married couples in marriage preparation is an important trend, but most need help to describe how sex functions in their marriages as a source of grace.

What children need more than anything else from their parents concerning sex is a sense of how a sexual relationship functions to draw their parents into loving relationships. Many troubled marriages could be helped without professional counsel if couples could learn to communicate better, especially in their sexual relationship. Pastoral ministers need to hear the woman who said of her experience: "Sexual lovemaking is like being spiritually fed; it is like going to communion."

5. *Strongly affirm God's plan for marriage and family life while showing acceptance and compassion for those who fail to live this ideal.* Today, it seems, we must constantly answer the question, "What do you do for yourself?" In contrast, Gabriel Marcel reminds us that a family "is not created or maintained as an entity without the exercise of generosity."

The family is a school of virtue that God sets before us, shaping and molding us to become people who learn to love and genuinely wish to share God's life of love. In the family, we lose our life, our grasping need to be someone, and then find ourselves by fulfilling our functions. Giving birth, and then nourishing and sustaining that new life require gifts of self-spending and generosity. Husbands and wives learn that in giving themselves fully to each other they forge a mutual bond of love that can be fruitful and creative. Mothers and fathers learn that in struggling with the demands of nurturing children they develop a love that goes beyond themselves. Children learn to flourish in a setting where they are loved unconditionally and find themselves recipients of a gift to which they have no rightful claim.

Anyone who upholds the ideal of the two-parent family may be ridiculed and dismissed today. We are warned against blaming single mothers and challenged to validate all family forms. Many judge the two-parent household far less critical to the healthy development of children than we previously believed. The Journal of Marriage and Family recently reviewed a book by taking the author to task for perpetuating "the misguided belief that children will receive better parenting in intact families."

While recognizing that two-parent families may not always be possible, and that many are dysfunctional while many non-traditional families are successful, can we at least say that two-parent families are generally best for children and spouses? Evidence certainly supports what most Americans still believe. Studies show that children from single-parent families and stepchildren are much more likely to have emotional and behavioral problems than children who have both biological parents in the home.

Self-gratification has surpassed self-sacrifice and Americans are much less willing to invest time and energy in family life. The value placed on children has dropped. Most adults do not seem to be more fulfilled. Deliquency, teenage suicide, and child abuse have proven worse in families without a mother or a father.

Non-traditional families can be successful and they deserve our sympathy and support, especially compassion in their brokenness. But evidence abounds that these families are not as successful as conventional two-parent families. Ask any child which kind of family he or she prefers. Ask any spouse about his or her desire for a stable, loving marriage, or any divorced person about a sense of failure. Look at God's plan in scripture. It is time we strive for a parish consensus on family values. We value families. We value marriage. We value children. We value parents. We are committed to a real concern for family life.

6. *Provide opportunities for Christian families to support and affirm one another.* Couples succeeding in marriage generally have a strong faith life and a good support system. Today we witness the outgrowth of support groups for abusive parents, families with children on drugs, couples hurt by adultery or marital problems, single-parents, and young mothers. Such support groups often emerge because traditional institutions do not meet members needs in an increasingly complex society.

Joan Hoxsey, a family counselor, says: "Traditionally, couples don't talk about the intimate details of their marriage with anybody, sometimes not even with each other, but especially not with other folks. They can talk about things like the house or the car, but not about values and issues of friendship. Couples need the support of other couples – to know what they are going through is probably not too different from the experience of others in general."*

The most stress-effective families make the most use of support systems. A 1981 study of family support systems by Nancy Coletta found that those parents with high levels of support were more affectionate toward, closer to, and more positive with their children, while those with low levels of support were more hostile to, indifferent toward, and rejecting of their children. John Paul II assured us in *Familiaris Consortio*: "The assistance from family to family will constitute one of the simplest, most effective and most accessible means for transmitting from one to another those Christian values which

---

* Quoted by Dan Morris, "Seasons of a Marriage: how to keep a good thing growing", *U.S. Catholic*, (September, 1988), p. 36.

are both the starting point and goal of all pastoral care" (FC, 69).

Despite the needs and benefits, support groups are rare. We neglect couples as they become married and need special help from those with experience, but we have been equally negligent of the need to nurture marriages at all stages. Couples facing decisions about issues such as children or handling conflict can get insight from other couples, which puts their anxiety into perspective and helps them realize they are likely making mistakes common to most families.

Families often let stresses build up rather than admit they need support. But don't blame families too readily. Few parishes sponsor support systems. More sponsor support groups for the separated and divorced. A ministry to total families and not just to individuals would be a new and vitally important mission for the parish.

7. *Healthy parishes will take a pastoral rather than a legal approach to marriage and family life.* The church has been strong on rules and guidelines that often limit or negate pastoral sensitivity toward couples requesting marriage, persons struggling in their relationships, or family events like baptism. People are too often turned away from the church by someone reading the rules, quoting canon law, or telling them they cannot be helped because they do not live within the parish boundaries. Couples are frequently refused sacraments because they fail to measure up to parish policies or diocesan guidelines.

Pastoral insensitivity presents a grave obstacle to continued practice in the church. When guidelines are upheld so rigidly that they become an excuse to deny Christian marriage or pastorally sensitive support, we appear to lack the spirit of the gospel. We frequently miss an opportunity to welcome an alienated or nominal Catholic couple and even deny their radical right to receive the sacraments. We create far too many barriers that block opportunities to reconcile and to evangelize.

The laity are becoming more vocal in their call for pastorally sensitive parish staffs. Families, who deal daily with reconciliation, often find the church harsh in its failure to reconcile. Parents, who honestly believe that young couples will eventually return to active practice in the church, find it difficult to understand why baptism is denied to a non-participating couple approaching the church in good faith.

We seem to have a double standard in the church. When a priest is struggling with his vocation, the church will send him for months of renewal. The same is true for religious. When the struggling parties are married, however, we are prone to judge them, perhaps with exhortations to get their act together. For all its condemnation of divorce, the church provides very little help for hurting couples. Why different treatment for different vocations when we now acknowledge that married couples truly live a vocation or call from God?

We expect priests and nuns to make an annual retreat for their spiritual health. Why not ask married couples to give at least one weekend each year to their spiritual growth? If we hope to truly care for couples living marriage, we need more weekend programs when most of the laity are away from jobs. One hour a week won't do any more good than a rushed Sunday liturgy. Much of the spiritual growth of our generation has happened through Cursillo, Marriage Encounter, Parish Renewal, Beginning Experience, and other groups with significant time for a conversion experience.

There's another problem. These renewal programs generally depend upon a priest as part of the team. The shortage of priests already makes it difficult to cover all of the Sunday Masses. Parishes would benefit if they settle for an occasional Sunday morning paraliturgy while their priest helps with retreats, Engaged Encounter, Retrouvaille, and other weekend programs that strengthen marriage and family life and develop future leadership. Sunday Mass is certainly important, but a renewal weekend can do more than 52 Sunday liturgies for true faith development.

The church is as guilty as any institution in pulling families apart. Parishes sponsor men's clubs and women's groups, involve family members in different liturgies, and invite individuals rather than couples to minister. The very nature of our programs, targeted for age and gender groups, single out individuals rather than invite family participation.

The question is whether or not we are serious about good pastoral care of the church's sacrament of marriage. If we accept the family as the fundamental church unit, then it makes ultimate sense to focus ministry on couples called to build these primary communities of faith and love.

8. *Family ministry builds on the experiences of people, not on dogmas and rules.* The church has long been skeptical of experience as a basis for faith. Yet God keeps revealing God's self to us all the time through such major life experiences as birth, death, love and war. We frequently need help to interpret these experiences. Family ministry can help people make sense of their daily life experiences.

For many years, church "shepherds" nourished, guided, and watched over the "sheep." The church's will and God's will were identical and the church's authority existed for people's own good. Many Catholics would be comfortable with a return to a church approaching life with ready-made answers, and many church staffs would be happy to minister in this structure.

With the change from a familial-communitarian society to a technological-individualistic society, we pay more attention to individuals than to relationships or family systems. While giving lip service to the family, we continue to create and deliver programs that compete with the family. Functions that once belonged to the family have been taken over by the church. For example, while the church stresses that religious education begins in the home, professional parish staffs communicate the message that the family gets their spiritual nurture at church. Parish ministers fail to see how family relationships are central to our relationship with God.

"Children learn what they live." We assimilate the values, norms and practices of our own family and use them to evaluate the values and behaviors of others. Dynamic factors in the family system enable the individual to quickly internalize new learning. Growth toward maturity involves questioning and searching. Children learn as their parents struggle with relationships. Parents learn as their children go through the various stages of development. In the family system, we first experience and learn the meaning of bonding and belonging with which we build healthy relationships. We learn security and trust that later help us in our relationship with God.

Family ministry builds best on reflective experiences rather than didatic content. CFM members first observe to get the facts, partially by reflecting on their experiences. They ask "Why?" as they judge, looking for consensus and possible action. Their goal is to effect change in the situation they have observed and reported on. Change stems from members' reflection on how to express God's word through actions. Peer ministries like the encounter movements build upon the sharing of personal stories to help others gain insight into their experiences.

Trusting their own thinking and experiences more than those of religious leaders, today's Catholics reflect a new hunger for roots and family bonds in their growing search for intimacy. We need intimacy in the church too. Until we stop avoiding each other for fear of control or getting hurt, we will never listen to each other and share our faith stories and insights openly.

When parish staff see the family caught in changing roles and lifestyle and confused by viewing marriage as a path toward self-fulfillment, waiting gets difficult. Yet, church workers sometimes contribute to the confusion. The notion that women's roles are restricted to the home, children, and household duties has at least implicitly been reaffirmed by the church, which needs a new appreciation of womens' contribution. The church has inadvertently supported the male abandonment or flight from family obligation. The church would best foster a searching attitude.

9. *Family ministers need and deserve adequate training built on their gifts and responsibilities.* The church too often operates on either the belief that lay persons do not have gifts for ministry since they are not ordained or professionally trained, or a belief that the skills for lay ministry come naturally. Yet, experience says otherwise. When the church began to actively recruit lay persons for religious education in the middle of this century, many active Catholics doubted their ability to teach the faith and needed catechist preparation. In the 1960s, when we began to include couples in marriage preparation, most felt inadequate even after 25 years of healthy marriage. Couples

are often unaware of their gifts or uncertain about sharing the way they live their relationship.

A key task in recruting family ministers lies in helping the couple to see that what they have done is transferable and a gift for ministry. Recruitment is enhanced when we prove we are about quality ministry, i.e., serious about what we are doing. Couples want to participate in something of value. The recruiter needs to tell couples how they will be helped to do good ministry. The training offered is significant. A four hour training says this ministry is insignificant and anyone can do it. No training program for family ministry should be less than one full weekend. Once people have experienced good training, they will be anxious for more.

Recruiters need a theology statement showing the parish has a vision which is goal oriented and has a sense of direction. Before people can act, they need to understand the issues. Then they will be able to see some goals or issues worthy of their effort and time. Part of training is to help people develop a vision which is beyond their present sense of church.

Training for family ministers should begin where the couples are at, respecting their natural helping capacity and skills, and building on the familiar ways they function informally. Experiential training is best, allowing volunteers a chance to practice their skills. A good training process will be participant-centered rather than leader-centered, allowing trainees to build upon their natural abilities rather than simply receive input from the leaders. Adults learn best when they are free to create their own responses to situations and can learn from one another.

An important goal of training is empowerment. Self confidence grows with practice and feedback on one's performance. People who question their abilities and whether they are suited for the task need affirmation. The trainer cannot empower people, they empower themselves. Empowerment happens when people discover their gifts and skills.

In too many programs, we train persons and then leave them to their own resources without support, consultation, and supervision. Support or consultation is helpful for continuing education, but also for affirmation and keeping people clear about their roles. Training enhances the quality of family ministries, strengthening care already being offered by peers.

10. *Family ritual and liturgy form a foundation for creating religious ritual and liturgy relevant to life.* In the family, especially in raising children, we are introduced to ritual. There are certain things we do before bedtime, ways we set the table or welcome guests to our home for an evening. In a world that is frequently threatening and beyond our control, rituals provide predictability and assurance.

The danger is that we see rituals as magic, unconnected with our daily lives, as we often do to the rituals surrounding the church's sacraments. People erroneously think a sacrament works on its own by virtue of some mysterious power inherent in the sacramental elements, not understanding how Christ uses the rite which expresses our faith to make himself present. This invites us to be passive, no longer celebrants but simply recipients.

While rituals help us to deal with the unknown, they do not allow us to control it. If we can teach ritual in our families as a human need, we are less likely to perceive religious rituals as a divine need or a way to control God. Our rituals are the human way we seek to touch and celebrate a God who is always present, saving and healing us. God does not need us to break bread in order to be present to us. Our ritual actions bring us closer to one another as the body of Christ.

Rituals provide a bonding. We are connected, if only for a moment, with all the others present as we sing our national anthem together. Rituals take us away from the isolation felt in our society, satisfying for the moment our human need for community. Rituals frequently bind us to a shared past.

The assembly, the gathering of the family or the community, is one of the essential ingredients in ritual. Family ritual is the foundation of all ritual. The simple rituals we develop around bedtime, mealtime, or holidays offer our children their first understanding of religious ritual.

Every ritual constitutes a valuable contribution to our sense of identity, security and belonging. Religious ritual attempts, more specifically, to deepen our sense of the sacred by offering us a way of experiencing and expressing what is otherwise incomprehensible. If we can affirm in our families the sacredness of simple things like homemade bread or bedtime moments, we will become free to discover the holy in every ritual in life and begin to appreciate all of life as prayer.

The sacraments are acts of the church that touch human beings at the crucial moments in their lives, acts with a sensible and recognizable guarantee of grace to human beings. They make real the essence of the church in concrete life at moments like birth, maturation, nurturing, pardoning, loving, and dying. A sacrament is not simply the rite. Its full realization presupposes a whole life that is opening to God, as a flower to light. Sacrament implies a process of conversion and searching for God. If individuals seek reconciliation and find pardon in the sacrament of penance, they should be signs of reconciliation amid the conflicts of family life. We prepare for the church's ritual and liturgy day by day in the way we live with each other.

11. *Ordinary men and women are searching for a spirituality based on their daily life as Christians.* All of us have a deep yearning inside that needs to be satisfied. Our hearts yearn for something beyond ourselves. "You have made us for yourself, Lord, and our heart can find no rest until it rest in you!" (Augustine). Our greatest need is for a spiritual awakening.

The notion of spirituality is frequently subject to misunderstanding. For some it means an unreal piety. For many it summons up a split between body and soul, between religious and secular life. Spirituality cannot be divorced from daily life, from lived experiences, interpersonal relationships, and real events. Consequently, interpersonal communication and the relationship expressed most deeply by sexual intimacy are the core of spirituality for a married couple.

The spiritual life takes human nature and relates it to the Divine Mystery. Family spirituality refers to a family's ongoing attempt to live its life in communion with God, aware of the real presence of Christ in their midst. Holiness is wholeness. The spiritual life involves the mind, the body, the spirit, the emotions, the whole of life. The movement of the Spirit unites us all, where we are, in the messiness of ordinary human life.

We frequently realize union with God through the act of loving another human unconditionally. When we can love in healthy ways, we learn to see God in the ones upon whom we concentrate the force of our energy. "Everyone who loves is begotten of God and has knowledge of God" (1 John 4:7).

Some elements for a spirituality based on the holiness of family life include:

• **Incarnational.** Christian spiritual life is concrete and personal, discerning the presence and movement of God in our sensual experiences and enfleshed bodily in each other.

• **Communal, Not Private.** Christian spirituality builds on relationships, not primarily on a Jesus and me experience. The family centered church invites members to participate fully in its life and mission, to be involved together in the work of Christ.

• **Eucharistic.** Jesus took the most ordinary parts of our life and the most ordinary actions – eating and drinking, touch, anointing with oil – and showed us how faith and the beauty and power of mystery are contained in ordinary things and actions. If we can believe bread and wine become the presence of Jesus, why can't we believe Jesus can be as present in our parenting, our hospitality, our sympathy, our listening, and our lovemaking?

• **Creative.** Being creative is one of the closest experiences of God, whether making a baby, knitting a sweater, or building a new relationship. We participate in God's creation when we are lifegiving in our relationships and activities.

• **Listening.** We strive to hear the movement of the Spirit in our lives. God speaks through our children, our spouse, and others, calling us to conversion and healing, to dependence on God's power rather than dominance and control of our own lives.

• **Attentive to the Paschal Mystery.** Jesus gave us a model for our spiritual life in his death and resurrection. Spouses promise to love each other in good times and through a serious illness or a conflict of interests. Relationships go through an ongoing cycle of life and death, of dying to self so that we might make the decision to love each other again.

• **Accepting of Need for Ongoing Healing.** We hurt each other. We are hurt by others. We participate in a sinful world of conflict, selfishness, oppression of women, failure to care for the elderly, dysfunctional behaviors. We need to accept, to forgive, to seek forgiveness, and to come to peace.

• **Oriented to Others.** It is no accident that the happiest people are the ones who truly give of themselves. Our children, the ill health of aging parents, and the needs of other families call for the offering of self promised in the Eucharist.

Thus the spirituality for couples and families will be based on living love to its fullest in the messiness and joys of family life, where people say they most find God.

12. *To say the people are the church implies they share in mission both in the internal church and in the world.* The nature of the church is mission. The family-centered church exists not only for the members' life together, but also to fulfill the mission to serve others. Tragically, the golden rule to "Love your neighbor as you love yourself" has almost been lost because of the way we fear each other in our violent society. The parish message has stressed personal behavior far more than mission.

Mission is intrinsic to a sense of vocation. The family is a community gathered to be sent out in service to others. If the church is a mission, the laity are on the front line of the church's life. The deeper the sense of God's call or presence in their lives, the deeper a family's sense of mission or purpose. Aware of God's love for them, they are ready to go beyond the family for something bigger than themselves.

Some families are into power, competition, and striving to get ahead. They try to raise children to be winners, to pursue wealth, possessions, success and the good life. Other parents want their children to care about others and to give of themselves. They tend to be more contented and satisfied with simplicity. They like people and like to extend themselves to others. Despite the emphasis in advertising on the good life, an increasing number of families are beginning to consider service to others as an important secondary purpose of family. The church's challenge for mission best be affirming and convincing.

As children from these families grow up, they tend to be caring and responsible persons because of what they learned at home. They tend to be empathetic and altruistic. They actively seek opportunities to help others. Their lifestyle reflects hospitality, service and simplicity. They are not as concerned about status, possessions and power as a sign of success. At the same time, their altruistic activity is shared and does not dominate their lives so that it takes them from each other.

Unfortunately, the hierarchical church took over the mission, denying the family its God-given mission. Professionally trained church leaders took over social action and service, operating with a we/they attitude which created a passive laity. Too often the focus of the gathered church became preoccupation with ecclesial structure and programs. Parishes should not be the busy center of focus for member's activities but the place where disciples are formed to carry out the mission beyond the church doors.

Rather than decry what is happening in society, including the breakdown of the family, pastoral leaders need to affirm, support, and promote the mission of the family. Families may be victims of what is happening in our society, but they also share concern and have learned gifts for healing and creating new life. A church in mission must keep the agenda and gifts of the family, our primary experience of church, in a central position.

For God All Things Are Possible

When Jesus answered the Pharisees' question about the permanence of marriage, he concluded: "For man it is impossible, but for God all things are possible." His listeners walked away in disbelief. The apostles, "completely overwhelmed" by Jesus' teaching, asked him how anyone could live up to this teaching. Jesus told them marriage and family life depend not simply upon human effort but upon God's grace.

The church has been criticized since Vatican II for lack of attentiveness and ministry to families. Navel-gazing on the internal life and renewal of the institution has surpassed attention to the family-centered church, despite official affirmation that family life is crucial to the body of Christ.

We have our paradigms and don't easily look at new ways to minister. Our best hope for family ministry lies in families grasping the sacramental nature of their life together and then helping other families. In past days families helped each other with building bees, threshing crews, medical care for the sick, and provisions for many needs that have now been turned over to professionals. When the church puts its energy into programs rather than into peer ministry, tremendous resources go unused.

For all the prophets of doom within the church, I find loving couples and faithfilled families excited about their call. For all the individualism engendered by our culture and by the church's asceticism, I find family members sacrificing for others, e.g., in the renewal movements. For all the search for meaning in our society today, I most often hear people speak of God's presence in the nurturing love of their families. For whatever I have noted here about our failures as church, it is indeed in our human brokenness I discover that what is impossible for us is still possible for God.